MOZART AND THE ENGLISH CONNECTION

MOZART

and

THE ENGLISH CONNECTION

by

JOHN JENKINS

cygnus arts

PUBLISHED IN THE UNITED KINGDOM BY
Cygnus Arts, a division of Golden Cockerel Press
16 Barter Street
London
WC1A 2AH

First published 1998

ISBN 1 900541 60 2
ISBN 0 8386

CATALOGUING-IN-PUBLICATION DATA

A catalogue record for this book is available from the British Library

Printed in the United Kingdom by Biddles Ltd, King's Lynn and Guildford

For Shelagh

❧ CONTENTS ❧

ILLUSTRATIONS

PREFACE

IN RECENT YEARS THERE HAS BEEN AN EVER INCREASING INTEREST IN MOZART, resulting in a large number of publications devoted to his music and his career. But one aspect of his life which has not received due attention is his relationship with England.

Mozart was eight years old when he arrived in London, and he lived there for fifteen months during the years 1764–65. Handel had died five years previously, and Johann Christian Bach together with Carl Friedrich Abel, a fellow German, had been appointed Court composers. It was a time when musicians of all kinds flocked to London, making it, musically, the most cosmopolitan city in Europe. As an impressionable child, Mozart imbibed the wide variety of music that the capital had to offer, and from this experience he cherished an affection for England which was to remain for the rest of his life. He went on to make English friends, he received invitations to return to London, and on several occasions he made known his intentions to do so. His feelings for this country are epitomised in a letter he wrote to his father in October 1782 on the occasion of British naval victories over the French: "For you know that I am an out-and-out Englishman".

As far as I am aware there is no other book dealing specifically with Mozart and the English apart from one written in German by C. F. Pohl in 1867. It provides much useful information but is concerned only with the early period in London. The present book encompasses the different phases of Mozart's life during which he had a chance to demonstrate his connection with England.

The first part describes the vibrant musical scene in the London of 1764–65 and how it influenced Mozart's subsequent career. Details are given of young Wolfgang's performances, his compositions during this time and the composers who influenced him, notably Johann Christian Bach. Particularly interesting are Leopold Mozart's account of his family's life in London, and their encounters with important historical figures of the period.

Mozart made his first journey to Italy at the age of fourteen to obtain first-hand experience of the musical compositions and performances, especially of opera, which had made the country dominant throughout Europe. Italy was full of English people, some of whom the Mozarts had encountered in London. Leopold Mozart recounts how he and his son met well-known people, such as the diplomat Sir William Hamilton and his gentle first wife, Catherine; expatriates, including Charles Stuart, 'The Young Pretender'; other young Englishmen, including one of the famous Beckford family, who were on the fashionable Grand Tour. They met the celebrated musicologist Charles Burney, whose critical reviews of Mozart appeared much later, and a boy prodigy, also fourteen, who was dear to Wolfgang's heart, the young Thomas Linley.

We move to Vienna at, perhaps, the happiest time of Mozart's life when he became close friends with four musicians, three from London and one from Dublin, who were directly involved with his music. One was an English soprano, Nancy Storace, for whom he wrote the central role of Susanna in *The Marriage of Figaro*, and with whom, it appears, he fell in love. Another of these friends, Thomas Attwood, was his only English pupil. His studies shed light on a little recognised aspect of Mozart's life— his role as a teacher. The third was Stephen Storace, who became the finest English composer of his time, and the fourth was the tenor, Michael Kelly, who also sang in the first *Figaro* and provides first hand information about Mozart's life in Vienna.

The last part of the book takes us to the time after Mozart's death. The visit of his English admirers Vincent and Mary Novello to the composer's surviving relatives and friends casts further light on Mozart's career. The final chapter discusses the influence of Mozart on English composers and traces the public response to his music from his death to the present day.

The sources consulted are set out in the bibliography, but throughout I have made frequent use of the extensive Mozart family correspondence, drawing especially upon Leopold's detailed descriptions of their life in London, as well as contemporary newspaper accounts and public records. Another essential source is O. E. Deutsch's *Documentary Biography of Mozart*, together with the later additions compiled by Cliff Eisen. As far as references to currency are concerned, any attempts on my part to give modern equivalent values must be regarded as being very approximate.

The emphasis has been to provide information for the general reader interested in Mozart, rather than to give a detailed analysis and evaluation of his music for scholars. It is hoped that the present account will bring us to an even closer understanding of this much-loved composer.

ACKNOWLEDGEMENTS

The sources of the illustrations are as follows: figures 1, 2, 9, by permission of the Trustees of the British Museum; figures 4, 10, 11, 12, by permission of the British Library; figures 3, 7, by courtesy of the National Portrait Gallery, London; figure 5, by permission of the Trustees of the Dulwich Picture Gallery; figure 6, by courtesy of the Blair Castle Collection, Perthshire; figure 8, by permission of the Victoria and Albert Picture Library.

ABBREVIATIONS

Burney   Charles Burney, *A General History of Music from the Earliest Ages to the Present Period*, 4 vols. (1776–89); ed. F. Mercer, 2 vols. (New York, 1935).

Deutsch   O. E. Deutsch, *Mozart: A Documentary Biography*, translated by E. Blom, P. Branscombe, and J. Noble, 3rd edn. (London, 1991).

Briefe   W. A. Bauer, O. E. Deutsch, and J. H. Eibl, eds., *Mozart. Briefe und Aufzeichnungen. Gesamtausgabe.* 7 vols. (Kassel, 1962–75).

K.   refers to the original Köchel edition of Mozart's works (1862).

K³.   refers to the 3rd Köchel edition (1937).

K⁶.   refers to the 6th Köchel edition (1964).

Letters   E. Anderson, ed., *The Letters of Mozart and his Family*, 3rd edn. (London, 1985).

PART ONE
Mozart in London

FIG. I. Leopold Mozart with his son Wolfgang and his daughter Nannerl. Engraved by Jean Baptiste Delafosse after Louis Carrogis de Carmontelle, 1764, and presented by Leopold Mozart to the British Museum. © *The Trustees of the British Museum.*

❦ CHAPTER I ❦
THE JOURNEY TO LONDON

ENCOURAGED BY THE WARM RECEPTION HIS CHILDREN HAD RECEIVED on their visit to Vienna at the end of 1762, Leopold Mozart set himself the task of promoting them on an extensive European tour which was to last nearly three and a half years, a large part of which would be spent in London.

His motives were mixed. He was undoubtedly interested in obtaining a good financial return and his letters to Lorenz Hagenauer, his landlord and friend in Salzburg, are full of minute details about the profit and loss account of the enterprise. In this respect he has been much criticised for exploiting his young children to the detriment of their health and well-being. On the other hand, the elder Mozart was an experienced musician and he had early recognised that in the case of Wolfgang, especially, he had a child of prodigious musical ability. To further their talents he was genuinely convinced of the need to extend the education of his two children in a way which was impossible in the narrow confines of provincial Salzburg, and, in the event, he was proved to be right.

Nevertheless, prolonged travel for a whole family, including two small children, was a formidable undertaking. No wonder Leopold wrote after his arrival in London, "I am now in a city which no one at our Salzburg court has ever yet dared to visit and which perhaps no one will ever visit in the future".[1] In our time it is not easy to appreciate just how appalling long journeys could be in the mid-eighteenth century. Carriages were ill-sprung, or suspended only by leather straps, and the poor state of the roads meant that the slow, jolting, swaying vehicles were very uncomfortable. Passengers were packed tightly together, especially in winter when they were muffled in many clothes, and long periods in the company of persons of dubious nature could be a nightmare. Accidents to the carriages often took place, wheels flew off, or horses bolted, sometimes leading to injury. Travel was slow and frequent stops had to be made at inns to rest and to change horses. Here the conditions varied from being tolerable to being revoltingly filthy, with lice-infested beds and rascally innkeepers. The inns were common sources of those scourges of the age, smallpox, typhus, and other devaſtating diseases. For all these reasons, as well as the need to keep up appearances, the Mozart family travelled in their own carriage and ſtayed at the beſt inns they could afford.

On 9th June 1763, Leopold Mozart, his wife, his son Wolfgang, aged seven, and his daughter Maria Anna (Nannerl), aged nearly twelve, together with their servant, set out from Salzburg on their long journey. They had not gone very far before the back wheel of their carriage broke into pieces and they were ſtranded outside the small Bavarian town of Wasserburg. Fortunately there were no injuries to the family, but they were delayed for two days before repairs could be made. In the meantime Leopold Mozart took his son into the church to see the organ. His father explained the use of the pedal and, in spite of the faƈt that Wolfgang had never used such an inſtrument before, Leopold writes:

he tried it ſtante pede, *shoved the ſtool away and played ſtanding at the organ, at the same time working the pedal, and doing it all as if he had been praƈtising it for several months. Everyone was amaᴢed. Indeed this is a fresh aƈt of God's grace, which many a one only receives after much labour.*[2]

The carriage repaired, they continued on their way to Munich. Here the children performed in three concerts before the Eleƈtor of Bavaria for which they were rewarded with the sum of 175 gulden, (about £1000).

Leopold Mozart's letters to his friend and landlord in Salzburg, Lorenz Hagenauer, provide us with fascinating details throughout the whole journey. It is clear from these letters that he was a paſtmaſter in the art of public relations, so necessary for the success of his enterprise. This involved working to an organised plan. Before moving on to a city he would firſt attempt to get letters of introduƈtion from ambassadors and other important people to highly placed members of society in that city, preferably members of a royal court. Having arrived and inſtalled his family in a good inn, he would then insert notices on several days in the local newspaper extolling the virtues of his children and advertising the dates of the concerts they would give. The place and the time were moſt important. If at all possible they were scheduled for the period during which the court and nobility were in residence, since it was this seƈtion of society that Leopold mainly relied upon for supporting his concerts. He dressed his children to the beſt of his ability and then the family ſtrolled in public to make sure their presence was known.

After Munich their journey continued westwards to Augsberg, Leopold's old home, but in spite of his plans and his local connections, he was disappointed in the lack of financial success that they achieved there.

An important objective was Mannheim where the orchestra under the leadership of Johann Stamitz (1717—57) had become renowned throughout Europe for a particular style, with its famous crescendo and juxtaposition of sharp contrasts, which set new heights of instrumental performance. In fact, the summer residence of the ruling Elector Palatine was nine miles outside Mannheim at Schwetzingen, and therefore Leopold stopped here on 13th July. This time the plan worked well. With letters of introduction from people in Vienna and Munich, Leopold was able to arrange a concert lasting four hours. They were financially well rewarded, but even more important for Wolfgang was his first encounter with the celebrated orchestra, and the Mannheim style was to have considerable influence on his future compositions.

The family then proceeded via Heidelberg and Mannheim to reach Mainz. From here they made a side trip by boat on the Rhine to Frankfurt-am-Main, where Wolfgang performed on the harpsichord and organ. The concert was attended by the fourteen-year-old Goethe who, in 1830 at age eighty-one, said "I still remember quite clearly the little fellow with his wig and sword".[3]

Returning to Mainz, they continued northwards to Coblenz. By now they had been travelling about three months, and in his careful financial appraisal of the enterprise Leopold calculated that so far they had spent 1068 gulden (about £6,000).

They then went on to Cologne and westwards to Aachen making for the Austrian Netherlands, but on their way to Liege a carriage wheel again broke and they were forced to stop at a small inn for repairs to be made. Here they sampled Dutch rural life. In his evocative style, Leopold Mozart wrote

we sat down on Dutch wicker chairs by the fireplace where a cauldron hung from a long chain holding meat, turnips, and all manner of other things all boiling together. We were given a miserable little tablecloth, and soup and fish were served to us, along with a bottle of red champagne. The door was left open constantly so that we frequently had the honour of a visit from the pigs, who grunted all around us. You can best envisage our midday meal if you imagine a Dutch painting.[4]

The coach repaired, they continued their journey reaching Brussels on 4th October. The family stayed six weeks in Brussels. Much of the time was spent waiting while Prince Charles, governor of the Austrian Netherlands, made up his mind to receive them. Here Leopold again displayed his knowledge of the visual arts by describing pictures by Rubens and many other artists that he had seen during their enforced stay in the city. Eventually they were able to give a performance before the nobility and were suitably recompensed. Leopold also describes how the children were constantly being given many valuable presents wherever they performed, including items like snuff boxes, watches, clothes, and swords, so much so that, as he cynically observes, "we shall soon be able to rig out a stall".

They finally left Brussels on 15th November and travelling via Mons they reached Paris three days later. Here they were welcomed to stay at the house of the Bavarian minister in Paris, the Count van Eyck and his wife, even being given the use of the countess's splendid harpsichord.

But Paris presented Leopold with a very different problem as far as the promotion of his children's talents was concerned. It was a large metropolis with no time for small town contacts, and he soon found that his letters of recommendation from such luminaries as the French ambassador in Vienna or the imperial ambassador in Paris, and from important people in Brussels were of no avail. But his salvation came from an unexpected quarter. He also had a letter of introduction from a Frankfurt merchant's wife to Friedrich Melchior Grimm (1723–1807). Grimm turned out to be a most important person in the intellectual life of the capital. Born in Regensburg, he studied in Leipzig and came to Paris in 1749, where he became secretary to the powerful Duc d'Orleans. A successful political writer, he became editor of the influential literary journal *Correspondance Littéraire*. Apparently, Grimm immediately befriended the Mozart family. Only twelve days after their arrival in Paris, his journal carried a long notice, dated 1st December 1763, about the Mozart children:

True prodigies are sufficiently rare to be worth speaking of, when you have had occasion to see one. A Kapellmeister of Salzburg, Mozart, by name, has just arrived here with two children who cut the prettiest figure in the world. His daughter, eleven years of age [actually twelve], *plays the harpsichord in the most brilliant manner; she performs the longest and most difficult pieces with an astonishing precision. Her brother, who will be seven years old next February* [actually eight in January], *is such an extraordinary phenomenon that one is hard put to it to believe what one sees with one's eyes and hears with one's ears".⁵*

The entry then goes on at great length to extol the musical talents of Wolfgang, emphasising not only his ability to perform at the keyboard but also his precocious skills as a composer.

But in order to succeed in Paris Leopold Mozart knew that it was necessary to be received by the king and queen, and at the end of December the family moved to Versailles where Louis XV, in the tradition of his predecessor, le Roi de Soleil, held court. On New Year's Day 1764, they finally received the royal summons and, dressed in their new black clothes, they appeared at a court dinner. The formality of the court etiquette struck Leopold forcibly: "It is not the custom here to kiss the hand of the royal persons or to disturb them with a petition or even to speak to them au passage, as they call it". It was therefore particularly pleasurable for Leopold to find that room was made for them all to go up to the royal table:

my Wolfgang was graciously privileged to stand beside the Queen the whole time, to talk constantly to her, entertain her and kiss her hands repeatedly, besides partaking of the dishes which she handed him from the table. I stood beside him, and on the other side of the King, where M. le Dauphin and Madame Adelaide were seated, stood my wife and daughter.⁶

Having been recognised by the king and queen, Leopold found that the doors of the nobility of Paris were opened to him. The children were able to give several performances and his initial fears about the financial success of their stay were allayed.

Their good fortune was undoubtedly due to the influence of Melchior Grimm and Leopold Mozart recognised this when he wrote:

He brought our business to court. He arranged for the first concert and he paid me on his own account eighty louis d'or, that is to say, he got rid of three hundred and twenty tickets. In addition he paid for the lighting, as more than sixty large candles were burnt.⁷

In view of these warm feelings it is sad, therefore, that fourteen years later, after his son had returned to Paris, the relationship between Wolfgang and Grimm became sour.

The family remained in Paris for five months. During this period editions of Wolfgang's own compositions were first published, four sonatas for harpsichord and violin, two of which (K.6, K.7) had been written in Salzburg and Brussels, and two (K.8, K.9) had been composed in Paris. Leopold could not conceal his pride when writing to his friend in Salzburg: "Picture to yourself the furore which they will make in the world when people read on the title-page that they have been composed by a seven-year-old child".[8]

Of the many musicians Wolfgang met in Paris the most influential were the German émigrés Johann Eckard (1735–1809), Leontzi Honauer (c. 1730–c. 90), Hermann Friedrich Raupach (1728–78) and, especially, Johann Schobert (1735–67). In 1767 Mozart made composite transcriptions of keyboard sonatas by these composers to form his first four piano concertos (K.37, K.39, K.40, K.41). Schobert wrote a large number of works for the keyboard as well as symphonies in a highly individualistic style, involving elements of passion and pathos, before his life was ended prematurely by eating poisonous mushrooms. Unfortunately, Leopold developed a personal animosity towards the eminent composer, whom he accused, somewhat improbably, of envy and jealousy of his daughter Nannerl's abilities. Despite his father's feelings, Wolfgang was greatly affected by Schobert, as is shown in his early keyboard sonatas. This influence was to persist even into his later works, such as the important Piano Sonata in A minor (K.310) where, for example, Schobert's use of the minor key and sense of pathos can be detected.

On 10th April 1764 the family said farewell to their good friend Melchior Grimm, who had done so much for them. At their departure he gave Nannerl a gold watch and Wolfgang a gold and silver knife. It was Grimm, together with others, including the English ambassador in Paris, the Duke of Bedford, who finally persuaded Leopold to go to England. Already, Wolfgang's musical genius had been enriched by what he had experienced during these last ten months. Much more was to come.

For the last stages on their journey to England, Leopold engaged a second servant, an Italian called Porta, who was familiar with the route. They reached Calais without incident. Confronted by the sea for the first time, Nannerl states with wonder in her diary "I saw how the sea runs away and comes back again".[9]

In the 1760s the regular cross channel service was by packet boats which sailed, weather permitting, three times a week, taking four to twelve hours, according to the sea conditions. Leopold Mozart elected to charter his own boat at a charge of five guineas, offsetting some of the cost by taking four other passengers. A further expense could be incurred by the frequent habit of the captain to stand offshore on arrival at Dover to avoid paying harbour dues. The passengers, as in the case of the Mozart family, were then rowed ashore in a small boat at extra cost to them. Leopold graphically describes the crossing: "Thank God we have safely crossed the channel. Yet we have not done so without making a heavy contribution in vomiting. But we saved money which would have been spent on emetics and thank God we are all well".[10]

Writing in his *Travels through France and Italy* in the year before the Mozarts arrived in England, Smollett commented, "Dover is commonly regarded a den of thieves. The people are said to live by piracy in time of war; and by smuggling and fleecing strangers in time of peace".[11] Leopold wholeheartedly confirms this view when he writes:

Whoever has too much money should just take a journey from Paris to London; for his purse will certainly be lightened. . . . As soon as you arrive at Dover it is even worse; and when you land from the boat you find yourself surrounded by thirty to forty people who are all "your most obedient servant" and who want to snatch your luggage from your own servants in order to carry it to the inn, after which they must be paid what they demand.[12]

However, their new servant, Porta, having done the journey many times before, proved to be quite capable of handling the importunate mob who surrounded them.

The road from Dover to London was, according to Smollett,

the worst in England with respect to the conveniences of travelling, and must certainly impress foreigners with an unfavourable opinion of the nation in general. The chambers are in general cold and comfortless, the beds paltry, the cooking execrable, the wine poison, the attendance bad, the publicans insolent, and the bills extortion.

He goes on to say "it would be for the honour of the kingdom to reform the abuses of this road; and in particular to improve the avenue to London by way of Kent Street [Old Kent Road], which is a most disgraceful entrance to such an opulent city".[13]

In addition to the unpleasantness of the services, the journey from

Dover could also be very hazardous since the road was a notorious haunt of footpads and highwaymen. In spite of this, the Mozarts appear to have survived the various perils without incident, and on 23rd April 1764 they crossed old London Bridge and entered the city.

CHAPTER II

THE MUSICAL SCENE IN LONDON, 1764–1765

B Y THE END OF THE SEVEN YEARS' WAR IN 1763, LONDON HAD BECOME the greatest city in Europe and the capital of a fast expanding overseas empire, with a population of three quarters of a million people. Riches flowed into the country on an unprecedented scale and in this period of prosperity the arts flourished. It was the age of Gainsborough and Reynolds, of Robert Adam and Capability Brown, of Chippendale and Wedgewood—men whose talents were supported not just by the old landed aristocracy but, more widely, by the wealth of a rapidly expanding middle class of merchants and members of the professions. Music took a prominent place in this enthusiasm for the arts. The greatest variety was to be found in London, and it was here, during 1764–65, that the Mozart family spent fifteen months immersed in English musical life.

It was ten months since little Wolfgang had left Salzburg. He had already gained much from his visits to places such as the court of Mannheim and Paris, but these experiences were nothing compared with those he would obtain in London.

In many respects the Mozarts would have found the musical scene in London to be very different from that of the rest of the continent. In England there was no system of narrow patronage confined to a royal court or the ruler of a small city state, as in Salzburg and other parts of Europe, so that musicians were free to come and go as they pleased. Because of the way in which wealth was distributed, financial support came from a far wider section of the population. The result was that the actual production of musical ventures was not subject to the whim of a rich patron but was entrepreneurial, in the hands of theatre or concert-hall managers.

Another noticeable feature was the cosmopolitan nature of the musicians. Since the death of Purcell in 1695 there had been no English composer of comparable stature. The absence of any native musical talent of major significance at a period when there was wide appreciation of overseas artists meant that foreign musicians flocked to England to earn their living. The outstanding example in the earlier part of the century had been Handel, whose overwhelming genius had dominated English music, often

9

to the detriment of contemporary composers. Even after his death in 1759 he remained the favourite composer of the king, and his oratorios, in particular, continued to feature prominently in the music programmes of the time.

The young King George III had come to the throne in 1760 and the following year married the twenty-one-year-old Princess Charlotte of Mecklenburg-Strelitz. In general, historians have not been kind to the young royal couple. George was woefully immature to be an effective ruler, and Charlotte was certainly no beauty, but they had one redeeming feature in common; both were ardent music lovers. The king had taken instruction on composition from Handel, and the queen was a competent singer and player of the harpsichord.

It is not very surprising that after the long reign of Handel the Hanoverian court continued with its preference for German masters by bringing Carl Friedrich Abel, composer of symphonies and exponent of the viol da gamba, from Dresden to become musician to the royal household. Then, in 1762, his more famous compatriot Johann Christian Bach, youngest son of the great Johann Sebastian, followed him at court; it was J. C. Bach who was to have a such a profound influence on the development of the young Mozart in London.

Opera

Then, as now, opera was a minority taste, albeit an important one. The vogue for Italian opera in England had begun early in the century particularly with the arrival of Handel, who was a was a great exponent of opera seria with its formal components of set-piece arias strung together by long recitatives to form the story, the libretto being usually about heroic characters from ancient legend. The appeal of these operas to a largely upper class audience was Handel's superb music and the opportunity to hear fine singers, particularly those essential to opera seria, the great castrati. Following his first success *Rinaldo* in 1711, Handel produced over thirty more operas for the London stage during the next three decades. By the end of this period, however, enthusiasm for his operatic works had waned to such an extent that he was in financial difficulties and thereafter he concentrated on oratorio.

The reasons for this change in tastes were several, but one important factor was the sudden popularity of English ballad opera and especially burlesque operas, such as *The Dragon of Wantley* (1737), with music by John Lampe and a libretto by Henry Carey, which deliberately caricatured Italian opera, so much so that for two out of the next three seasons there was no Italian opera at all.[1]

Nevertheless, Italian opera continued to attract a select audience and it still brought many Italian composers and virtuosi to this country. But by the 1760s musical composition had changed considerably. The baroque form of Handel was forsaken for the fashionable Italianate galant style. At the King's Theatre the season ran from November to May. According to that highly informative eighteenth-century music critic, Charles Burney, writing in his *General History of Music*, there were seven new Italian operas performed in London during the 1764–65 season, most of which are also listed by Leopold, and which his son would have attended.[2] Many are now of interest to music historians only, but one has associations with Mozart — the pasticcio opera *Ezio*, which began the season on 24 November 1764. Pasticcio, a popular form at the time, consisted of an opera assembled from arias contributed by several composers, using either an old or newly written libretto. For *Ezio*, J. C. Bach contributed an aria, 'Non so d'onde viene', which so impressed the boy Mozart that many years later he wrote his own version. *Ezio* is also memorable for the fact that when Mozart was in London he composed his first aria, 'Va, dal furor portata', K.21, using the text from the opera.

On 1st January 1765 there was another pasticcio, *Berenice*, which included a march by Abel and a popular aria by Bach. Then on 26th January, to great anticipation and by royal command, Bach presented *Adriana in Siria*, the third opera he had composed since his arrival in England. The subject was Hadrian's campaign in Syria and his suppression of the Jewish uprising, with a favourite libretto by Metastasio. It prompted Horace Walpole to write, "our last three Saturdays at the opera have been prodigious and a new opera by Bach last night was so crowded that there were ladies standing behind the scenes during the whole performance".[3] In spite of a fine cast, the anticipation aroused by this work was not borne out in the event, and Charles Burney states,

whether from heat or inconvenience, the unreasonableness of expectation, the composer being out of fancy, or too anxious to please, the opera failed. Everyone seemed to come out of the theatre disappointed, and the drama was performed but two or three times.[4]

The programme was continued on 2 March with *Demofoonte* by the Neopolitan composer Matteo Vento (1735–76) who had arrived in England soon after Bach and continued to compose and teach the harpsichord here until his death. Burney said of the opera that it "was natural, graceful, and pleasing; always free from vulgarity, but never very new or learned".[5]

Another celebrated Italian composer to settle in England at this time was Felice Giardini (1716–96).[6] He was such a fine violinist that Burney regarded his arrival in 1750 as marking the beginning of "a memorable aera in the instrumental Music of this kingdom".[7] As a composer he was partly responsible for introducing the modern light Italian style to London and as leader of the orchestra at the King's Theatre he insisted on new standards of playing. In the early 1760s Gainsborough painted a fine portrait of Giardini and the two became well acquainted.[8] A letter written by the painter displays his enthusiasm for music when he says,

You put me in mind of a little fiddle that Giardini pick'd up here in Bath, which nobody would think well of, because there was nobody who knew how to bring out the tone of, and which . . . in his hands produced the finest music in the world.[9]

On 7th March 1765, Giardini gave the next opera in the season, *Il re pastore*. (It is of interest that, ten years later, the same libretto of this work, by Metastasio, would be set to music by Mozart himself). April 27th marked the opening of *Olimpiade* by the English composer Thomas Arne (1710–88). This was his only essay into Italian opera. It was not a success and was criticised scathingly by Burney,

But the doctor had kept bad company; that is he had written for vulgar singers and hearers, too long to be able to comport himself properly at the Opera-house in the first taste and fashion. . . . [T]he common play-house and ballad passages, which occurred in almost every air in his opera, made the audience wonder how they got there.[10]

It failed after only two performances.

In recent years there has been an increasing appreciation of English composers of the eighteenth century, and of these Thomas Arne is undoubtedly one of the more accomplished. The son of an upholsterer in Covent Garden, Arne studied with the Italian composer Francesco Geminiani (1677–1762), who had settled in London in 1714. His first success was the masque *Comus* (1738), followed in 1740 by another masque *Alfred*, which ends with his best-remembered song 'Rule Britannia'. Thereafter, over the next thirty-six years, his prolific output included thirty operas of which his masterpiece is *Artaxerxes* (1762). This is an opera seria in the Italian manner but sung in English, the libretto by Metastasio being translated by Arne himself. Its success was due to the quality of the music and its sense of dramatic effect, fine orchestration and the use of top singers in the main roles, of the calibre of John Beard, Charlotte Brent and the castrato Tenducci. Apart from *Artaxerxes* none of Arne's operas have survived, and remarking on them Burney says

the number of his unfortunate pieces for the stage was prodigious; yet none of them were condemned or neglected for want of merit in the Music , but words, of which the doctor was too frequently guilty of being the author.[11]

Possessed of an irascible temperament which brought him into conflict with most of the English theatre managers of the time, Arne was an erratic composer. At his best, he compares favourably with many of his European contemporaries and he was able to keep abreast of the new galant style which had swept into England since the death of Handel. Now he is better remembered for his instrumental music and some of his songs. He and his much less-regarded son, Michael, met the Mozart family and are recorded by Leopold Mozart in his travel notes. The season at the King's Theatre ended in May 1765 with the pasticcio *Solimano*, which appears to have made no impact.

Italian opera was favoured especially by higher society and the intelligentsia, but for a much wider audience there were the rival attractions of English opera. During 1764–65, productions at Covent Garden included a revival of Arne's *Artaxerxes*, a new comic opera, *The Guardian Outwitted*, also by Arne, and a pastiche comic opera, *The Maid of the Mill*, arranged by the composer Samuel Arnold (1740–1802), with contributions by J. C. Bach and other composers. Arnold went on to write over forty English operas, but much of the music is quite unmemorable.

At Drury Lane, in November 1764, attempts to compete with *Artaxerxes* led to the staging of *Almena*, an English Italianate opera seria, in part by the younger Arne, and this was followed later in the month by a full-length opera, *The Capricious Lovers*, by George Rush (fl. *c.* 1760–80) who had already written a serious English opera, *The Royal Shepherd*, earlier in the year. In spite of his documented operas and his instrumental compositions, little is known of Rush's career although Leopold Mozart refers to meeting the composer "Mr Ruff".[12] In February 1765 the Drury Lane season continued with *Pharnaces*, an opera seria in English, by William Bates (fl. *c*.1750–80) who also wrote songs and instrumental music, but, like Rush, is a composer about whom little is known and is now almost totally forgotten.

Undoubtedly the most popular production by far in the early part of the eighteenth century was that phenomenal success, *The Beggar's Opera*, first produced by John Gay in 1728. It was to have a profound effect on operatic audiences in England. This was the original 'ballad opera', composed largely from a series of traditional songs, with a bitingly satirical libretto dealing with London's low life. There were many subsequent ballad operas, although none survived for very long. It was the advent of the ballad opera that led to the emergence of English comic opera, which had a much wider appeal than the old-fashioned Italian opera seria. Such was the enthusiasm for *The Beggar's Opera* that performances were given every season at both English theatres. It continued to draw large audiences throughout the eighteenth century and beyond, to be brought up to date in our own time by Bertold Brecht and Kurt Weill as the *Threepenny Opera*. Still more recently it has been the subject of an excellent arrangement by Benjamin Britten.

Oratorio

Apart from opera there was another aspect of vocal music which continued to be a great favourite with the English—oratorio. Here the works of Handel remained supreme, despite attempts by Arne and others, such as John Christopher Smith (1712–95) and John Stanley (1712–86), to produce their own. Much the best of these is *Judith*, which was composed by Arne in 1761 just before *Artaxerxes*. A performance of *Judith* was given in 1764 at the Lock Hospital, but, since Arne's death, it has been unjustly neglected. With the exception of Ash Wednesday, oratorios were produced at Covent Garden on Wednesdays and Fridays in Lent when plays and operas were forbidden; from 22nd February to 29th March 1765 there were no less than eleven performances of Handel's oratorios, including two of *Messiah*.[13]

The Singers

Managers of Italian opera considered that their music could only be sung satisfactorily by Italians. Another important factor contributing to the presence of Italian singers in Britain was the eighteenth-century predilection for the castrato. The conventions of opera seria dictated that the main male singers should be castrati, who, of course, were not native to England. In this country the castrato was an object of curiosity, which was mixed with admiration for his superior vocal technique. Lydia Melford, in Tobias Smollett's *Humphrey Clinker*, sums up the public's feeling about castrati when she says,

I heard the famous Tenducci, a thing from Italy—It looks for all the world like a man, though they say it is not. The voice, to be sure is neither man's nor woman's, but it is more melodious than either, and it warbled divinely, that while I listened I really thought myself in paradise.[14]

Ferdinando Tenducci (1736–90), a celebrated soprano castrato with the Italian opera ensemble, arrived in England in 1758 and became friends with the Mozarts when they were in London. In addition to the season's performances at the King's Theatre he performed regularly at the Ranelagh Pleasure Gardens and was closely associated with J. C. Bach, who wrote a series of song arrangements for him. He spent 1765–68 in Ireland where, somewhat surprisingly, he eloped with a rich, young pupil named Doris Maunsell. His portrait was painted by Gainsborough,[15] and Mozart subsequently wrote an aria for him (now lost) when they met again in Paris in 1778.

One of the highlights of the 1764–65 London season, which rescued Italian opera from the financial doldrums into which it had recently sunk, was the arrival of the famous male soprano Giovanni Manzuoli (*c.* 1720–1782) from Florence. Then, as now, well-known singers of international repute could command very high fees. Such was the star quality of Manzuoli that, according to Leopold Mozart, writing enviously in February 1765, he was being paid £1500 in advance for the season, as well as receiving the enormous sum of one thousand guineas (about £50,000 in present terms) for a single benefit performance of the opera *Il re pastore*.[16] At his inaugural performance in *Ezio*, Burney reports,

there was such a crowd assembled at all avenues that it was with very great difficulty I obtained a place, after waiting two hours at the door. Manzuoli's voice was the most powerful and voluminous soprano that had been heard on our stage since the time of Farinelli.[17]

He performed in all the Italian operas of that season to great acclaim whatever the merits of the opera. It was during this year in London that Manzuoli, after meeting the Mozarts, was so entranced by the young Wolfgang that he took the trouble to give the boy free singing lessons. This instruction from a master in vocal technique was to prove invaluable to Mozart in his first attempts at opera composition only two years later.

The Italian female singers of this period were regarded by the critics much less highly. They included Teresa Scotti who was described by Burney as having "an elegant figure, a beautiful face, and a feeble voice, but though in want of power she possessed great flexibility and expression" and Clementina Cremonini, "a good musician, with a modern style of singing, but almost without voice".[18] It was she who provided the vocal part in two of Mozart's London concerts.

English singers were not usually tolerated in the Italian opera, but one who did regularly perform in the King's Theatre because she was much better than her Italian counterparts was Mary (Polly) Young (1739–99), a niece of Mrs Arne.

But the most celebrated of the female singers at this time was in English opera. She was the soprano Charlotte Brent (1735–1802), a pupil and mistress of Thomas Arne. She had had a rapturous reception at her 1759 debut as Polly in *The Beggar's Opera*, which she continued to sing with great success, as well as most of the other important roles in opera and oratorio. She and all these other virtuosi were duly recorded in Leopold Mozart's travel notes.

The Theatres

In the middle of the century there were two theatres which were licensed to stage plays and opera with English dialogue. They were Drury Lane, and the larger Covent Garden, which had a capacity of about 2,100. There was also the Little Theatre in the Haymarket on the site of the present Haymarket Theatre, although it was not until 1767 that this theatre received a limited licence to perform English productions. Previous to this date the Little Theatre was mainly used for concerts and other entertainments. It was here on 21st February 1765 that Wolfgang Mozart and his sister gave a benefit concert. Finally, there was the King's Theatre, also in the Haymarket, which staged Italian opera only.

The English theatres were primarily concerned with plays, but at Covent Garden the manager was John Beard (c. 1717–91), a renowned tenor who had sung with great distinction in many of Handel's later oratorios. Beard steadily increased the proportion of operas in the theatre's repertoire. At Drury Lane, David Garrick (1717–79), the famous actor, was in charge and here fewer operas were staged.

The manager of the King's Theatre during 1764–65 was Felice Giardini, and the role of leader of the orchestra was taken by the French violinist, Francois-Hippolyte Barthélemon, who had arrived from Paris in 1764. Barthélemon, who was to marry the English soprano Polly Young, took an active part in London musical life as a violinist and as a composer of stage and instrumental works. He also composed several hymn tunes of which one, 'Awake my soul', is still well known today. In May and June Giardini and Barthélemon were billed to perform in concert with the child prodigy Mozart.

In many respects conditions in the theatres were very different from those of today. Performances started at six in the evening and there were no reserved seats. To avoid an undignified scramble or a long wait, places for the gentry were kept by their servants. Seat prices ranged from one and two shillings in the gallery to five shillings in the boxes. The whole floor of the theatre was occupied by the pit at a cost of three shillings. It was mainly frequented by young men of fashion. By modern standards the behaviour of the audience was often very unruly. The top gallery was frequently noisy. As Horace Walpole writes about his attendance at the opera *Ezio*, "the dances were not only hissed off, as they deserved to be, but the gallery, a-la-Drury Lane, cried out 'off! off!'".[19] During the interval the young bloods in the pit would sometimes gain access to the stage to visit the female performers and had to be ejected as the curtain rose. In the upper boxes prostitutes openly plied their trade, and even in the lower boxes, which were mainly occupied by the gentry, it often appeared that the clientele came more to be seen than to see the production. Then there was a constant risk of fire since productions were lit on the stage by several chandeliers of candles. But while stage lighting could be altered by raising and lowering the chandeliers, there was no way in which the house lights could be dimmed during the performance.

The Concerts

It was of course the concert scene which occupied much of the attention of Leopold Mozart since this is where his children would perform.[20] Concerts were usually mixed vocal and instrumental performances. They often took the form of benefit concerts in which the main performer paid all expenses and retained any profits, or they were by subscription, when the audiences paid for a whole series. The most famous from 1764 to 1782 were those directed jointly by C. F. Abel and J. C. Bach. The first of the Bach-Abel concerts was held at the Great Room, Spring Garden, on a site between what is now Cockspur Street and Horseguards Parade near St James's Park. According to a contemporary account, these rooms were most lavishly decorated in white and gold with a painted ceiling and were lit with many chandeliers. It was here that the Mozart children had their first public London performance in June 1764.

In January 1765 the Bach-Abel concerts were transferred to the Carlisle Rooms, at what is now Sutton Place, Soho Square, which was then an area of considerable social distinction. The programmes consisted almost entirely of Bach and Abel's own works and they were directed alternately by the two. The subscription for a series of six concerts was five guineas for gentlemen and three guineas for ladies. These not inconsiderable sums were obviously for the wealthier members of society, but for several years these Soho Square concerts, held every Wednesday, proved to be very successful in attracting a fashionable and exclusive audience, which included royalty. There is no evidence that the Mozart children actually performed here, but they attended the concerts, where the instrumental works of Bach and, to a lesser extent, of Abel, would have made a deep impression on the young Wolfgang. It is also clear from Leopold Mozart's notes that they were acquainted with the colourful owner of the Carlisle rooms, Mrs Theresa Cornelys (1727–97).[21] Born Theresa Imer, in Venice, she had married an actor named Pompeati and became an opera singer, making her first appearance in London in 1746. Burney was not very complimentary about her singing: "the Pompeati, though nominally second woman, had such a masculine and violent manner of singing, that few female symptoms were perceptible".[22] She returned to the continent, and in Venice in 1753 she renewed an old acquaintance with Casanova. She met him again in Holland, where he acknowledged that she had borne him a daughter, but while in Amsterdam she formed a liaison with a wealthy Dutchman and finally returned to England in 1760 with the name Mrs Cornelys. She took the title role in Arne's oratorio *Judith* in February 1761 and it was about this time that she erected and lavishly decorated the rooms next to Carlisle House. Fanny Burney, in her diary, writes glowingly of her visit in April 1770: "we went to Mrs Cornelys' with papa. . . . The magnificence of the rooms, splendour of the illumination and embellishments and the brilliance of the company exceeded anything I ever before saw".[23] For ten years Mrs Cornelys was a very successful impresario in the musical life of London, but disaster came in 1771 when she unwisely attempted to stage operas. She was prosecuted at the instigation of the owners of the powerful Italian Opera House and fined. Worse was to follow because shortly afterwards she was indicted for keeping a common disorderly house—an ironic charge when at that time the upper boxes of the opera houses were notorious haunts of prostitutes. In 1772 a magnificent rival establishment, the Pantheon, opened in Oxford Street, and Mrs Cornelys became bankrupt. She died in the Fleet prison in 1794.

In the same vicinity was another favourite concert hall, Hickford's Great Room, built by a Mr John Hickford in 1738. Its main entrance was in Brewer Street, near Piccadilly Circus, and there was a back entrance in Great Windmill Street where the sedan chairs of the wealthy patrons were instructed to wait. It was here that the Mozart children performed their last benefit concert in London on 13th May 1765. The building continued to exist until 1934, when it was demolished and the site was taken by part of the Regent Palace Hotel.[24]

Private Concerts

Quite apart from their attendance at the expensive subscription concerts, members of the nobility and gentry were able to assert their social status musically by holding concerts in their own homes for the privileged few. In 1764 Mrs Harris wrote to her son, "We are now very busy in preparing for our concert Wednesday morning, and I am greatly afraid there will be too great a crowd; however it will be of good company".[25] Often the performers were amateur musicians of the household; added sophistication was provided by hired professionals. Even the top virtuosi would perform, if the host was wealthy enough to pay their fees. A few years later Fanny Burney wrote, "On Thursday morning we went to a delightful Concert at Mr Harris's. The sweet Rauzzini was there and sung four Duets with Miss

Louisa Harris".[26] Leopold Mozart stated his intention of taking advantage of this source of income for his children when, on 13th September 1764, he wrote,

During the coming months I shall have to use every effort to win over the aristocracy and this will take a lot of galloping round and hard work. But if I achieve the object which I have set myself, I shall haul in a fine fish or rather a good catch of guineas.[27]

That he succeeded in his object is likely from the number of aristocratic names he mentions in his notebook.

The Music Societies

So great was the demand for musical entertainment that in addition to the designated concert rooms other venues were used. Several societies had been founded in the earlier part of the century to perform music, often to a high standard, with members of the Italian opera taking part. They included the Academy of Ancient Music, meeting fortnightly in the Crown and Anchor tavern, Arundel Street, near the Strand, and the Castle Concerts, so called because they had first met at the Castle Tavern in Paternoster Row. Later, in 1761 came the Noblemen and Gentlemen's Catch Club, which met at the Thatched House inn, St. James's Street, Piccadilly. Among its founders whom Leopold Mozart subsequently met, were men-about-town, Lords Eglinton and March. James Boswell, who was a friend of both, described his introduction to this form of entertainment in 1763, "I began singing catches, which is really a most entertaining thing. There is some lively sentiment well accompanied with suitable music, and when sung in parts a fine harmony is produced".[28]

The Pleasure Gardens

The most popular, and inexpensive, musical entertainments were to be found in the pleasure gardens of Marylebone, Vauxhall and Ranelagh, which were frequently attended by the Mozart family. It was here that a wider public showed its musical preference was for song. Instrumental concerts were held there, but for the majority vocal music had the most appeal. The emphasis was on attractive melody with straightforward, easily understood words. The composers of the day produced a stream of songs for the pleasure gardens. Many of them were of a pastoral nature, much liked at the time, of which Arne's 'Where the Bee Sucks' taken from his music for *The Tempest* is a lasting example. But, inspired by the recent British naval successes, there was also a great number of patriotic songs, such as the well known 'Heart of Oak' by the Master of the King's Musick, William Boyce (1711–79). More unexpected was the popularity of Scottish songs. This fondness for arrangements in the idiom of traditional Scottish airs dates back to 1725 when William Thomson, a Scot, published *Orpheus Caledonus*, a volume of fifty songs based upon Scottish texts by Allan Ramsay, father of the portrait painter. The vogue continued until the end of the century and collections were produced by many eminent composers, including Bach, Arne, and, later, Haydn. Many of the songs for the pleasure gardens were, however, ephemeral, lasting but one season, since the public constantly demanded new additions to the repertoire.

The smallest of the three main gardens was Marylebone, which had been opened for musical entertainment in 1738. It was located on a site which extended from what is now upper Wimpole Street to the streets to the west of Marylebone High Street. By 1764 the garden's leading singers were the manager of the gardens, the tenor Thomas Lowe, and his pupil, the soprano Anne Catley. For many years the Marylebone area had been a haunt of highwaymen; in *The Beggars Opera* Captain Macheath is made to say "There will be deep play tonight at Marylebone, and consequently money may be picked up on the road". Mr Lowe was thus forced to provide bodyguards for visitors to his gardens. However, Marylebone did not attract the same audiences as its larger rivals, and although the quality of the music was often good, Lowe sometimes felt the need to spice the concerts with fireworks. Fanny Burney's eponymous Evelina, visiting the gardens a few years later, says, "I had the pleasure of hearing a concerto on the violin by Mr Barthélemon who to me seems a player of exquisite feeling and variety. . . . The firework was really beautiful".[29]

The oldest of the pleasure gardens was Vauxhall on the Surrey side of the Thames, founded in the seventeenth century. It was frequently visited by Pepys: "Thence by water to Foxhall, and there walked an hour alone, observing the several humours of the citizens that were there this holiday".[30] It was restored in 1732, a bandstand was installed, and its riverside site remained a popular favourite for musical entertainment and refreshment during summer. Arne, in particular, produced a great deal of music for Vauxhall, publishing a set of songs every year for twenty years until 1766. Later he was joined by James Hook (1746–1827) and J. C. Bach, who wrote three collections of English songs specially for the audiences there. James Boswell waxes enthusiastically about the Vauxhall pleasure gardens:

that excellent place of public entertainment—it is peculiarly adapted to the taste of the English nation; there being a mixture of curious show, gay exhibition music, vocal and instrumental, not too refined for the general ear; for all of which only a shilling is paid; and though last, but not least, good eating and drinking for those who choose to purchase that regale.[31]

Lydia Melford, in *Humphrey Clinker*, talks of the pleasures of Vauxhall,

which I no sooner entered, than I was dazzled and confounded with the variety of beauties that rushed all at once upon my eye. Image to yourself a spacious garden, part laid out in delightful walks, bounded with high hedges and trees, and paved with gravel; part exhibiting a wonderful assemblage of the most

FIG. 2. The Chinese House, the Rotunda and the Company in Masquerade in Ranelagh Gardens, 1759, by John Bowles. © *The Trustees of the British Museum.*

picturesque and striking objects, pavilions, lodges, groves, grottoes, lawns, temples, and cascades; porticoes, colonades, and rotundos; adorned with pillars, statues, and painting; the whole illuminated with an infinite number of lamps, disposed in different figures of suns, stars, and constellations; the place crowded with the gayest company, ranging through those blissful shades, or supping in different lodges on cold collations, enlivened with mirth, freedom, and good humour, and animated by an excellent band of music.[32]

However, fashionable society more often frequented Ranelagh, which had opened in 1742. These gardens were situated in what are now the grounds of the Royal Chelsea Hospital and were laid out with a series of walks, incorporating grottoes and arbours and a canal where outdoor entertainments and elaborately staged masquerades were given. A central feature of the gardens was a large, beautifully-decorated amphitheatre, the Rotunda, with a central bandstand and two tiers of boxes round the periphery of a promenade where well-to-do members of society could show themselves. Here, indoor concerts started in April and continued three times a week until the end of August. Boswell also liked Ranelagh: "I felt a glow of delight at entering again that elegant place. This is an entertainment quite peculiar to London. The noble Rotunda all surrounded with boxes to sit in and such a profusion of well-dressed people walking round is very fine".[33] It was frequently used for high-class concerts where one could hear such celebrated singers as Charlotte Brent and Tenducci, who composed some of his own songs. Always seeking an entrée to society to promote his enterprises, Leopold Mozart realised the value of Ranelagh as a venue for important people, and in June 1764 the young Wolfgang was allowed by his father to take part in a charity concert given there in aid of a hospital foundation.

This was the rich musical scene which enthralled the little Austrian boy and his family after their arrival in London spring 1764.

❧ CHAPTER III ❧
PERFORMANCES IN LONDON

LEOPOLD'S NETWORK OF CONTACTS WITH INFLUENTIAL PEOPLE HAD ENSURED that the news of his children's successes in continental Europe preceded them to London. On 27th April 1764, only five days after their arrival, they were received by King George and Queen Charlotte at Buckingham House, where the children gave a performance. As they left they were duly rewarded with twenty-four guineas.[1]

After the stuffiness and indifference that they had greeted them on their arrival in Paris, Leopold found the openness of English society very refreshing. He was particularly impressed with the friendliness of the king and queen. He recounts how one week after their meeting, while they were walking in St James's Park, they met the king and queen riding in their carriage. The royal couple immediately recognised them, and the king, opening a window of the carriage, leaned out and waved a greeting "especially to our Master Wolfgang"

Only three weeks later they were again invited to Buckingham House to perform for the king and queen. The only other members of the audience were two brothers of the king and Prince Mecklenburg, the queen's brother. On this occasion Leopold gives more details of the performance. Wolfgang played on the organ as well as the harpsichord works handed to him by the king, which included music by the Viennese composer Wagenseil, the court composers J. C. Bach and C. F. Abel as well as the revered Handel. He played all these scores at sight, to great acclaim. He then accompanied the queen in an aria which she sang. "Finally," Leopold continues, "he took the bass part of some airs of Handel (which happened to be lying there) and played the most beautiful melody on it and in such a manner that everyone was amazed".[2]

For the royal performance they again received the fee of twenty four guineas, but it was time that a financially rewarding public appearance was staged. Accordingly, this was billed in the *Public Advertiser* for 17th May at Hickford's Great Room, Brewer Street, as part of a benefit concert for the cello virtuoso Carlo Graziani, and in company with the violinist, composer and manager of the King's Theatre, Felice Giardini, as well as the Italian opera singers Angiola Sartori, Clementina Cremonini and Antonio Mazziotti. Unfortunately, it had to be postponed because not all the soloists were available until 22nd May, but in the event Mozart was taken ill and was unable to appear.[3]

As Leopold sadly remarks, the summer months were very unfavourable to mount such enterprises since at this time of year most of the nobility, upon whose support he depended, left London for their country retreats.[4] Nevertheless, with perspicacity, Leopold noted that 4th June was the king's birthday when many of the well-to-do would be in town, and he therefore arranged a concert for the children to perform on the following day. The *Public Advertiser* for 31st May 1764 carried the following notice:

At the Great Room in Spring Garden, near St. James's Park, Tuesday, June 5, will be performed a grand Concert of Vocal and Instrumental Music. For the Benefit of Miss MOZART of eleven, and Master MOZART of seven Years of Age, Prodigies of Nature; taking the Opportunity of representing to the Public the greatest Prodigy that Europe or that Human Nature has to boast of. Every Body will be astonished to hear a Child of such tender Age playing the Harpsichord in such a Perfection—It surmounts all Fantastic and Imagination, and it is hard to express which is more astonishing, his Execution upon the Harpsichord Playing at Sight, or his own Composition. His Father brought him to England, not doubting but that he will meet with Success in a Kingdom, where his Countryman, that late famous Vertuoso Handel, received during his Life-time such Particular Protection. Tickets, at Half a Guinea each; to be had of Mr Mozart, at Mr Cousin's, Haircutter, in Cecil Court, St Martin's Lane.[5]

In this promotional exercise Leopold was not above stretching the truth by subtracting a year from the children's ages and to heighten the impact further he played upon the public's known affection for Handel.

A later announcement states that other artists would include Miss Cremonini, the King's Theatre soprano, and Francois Barthélemon, the violinist, also of the King's Theatre. It is not known exactly what the children played, apart from the mention of Wolfgang's own compositions. At this time, his published works consisted of the four sonatas for the keyboard with optional violin accompaniment (K.6–K.9) which had appeared in Paris and it is likely that these formed part of the programme. A letter from Leopold Mozart to Lorenz Hagenauer in Salzburg gives interesting details about the financial aspects of the concert. He states that the hire of the hall coſt him five guineas, two harpsichords were each half a guinea to rent, and the principal soloiſts each charged three to five guineas. There was an audience of over two hundred and the profit from this benefit concert amounted to more than ninety guineas—the present equivalent of about £4500.[6] Despite his worries, Leopold was very gratified that so many people attended the concert, including important members of the nobility such as the Earl of March, a close friend of James Boswell. It is a pity that Boswell himself had left London for the continent only eight months before the Mozarts arrived, otherwise we might have been treated to an entertaining description of their presence.

Three weeks later on 29th June came Wolfgang's next public performance, this time at a charity concert at Ranelagh in aid of a new maternity hospital for London. This was to be the Weſtminſter New Lying-in-Hospital, founded in 1765 on the Surrey side of Weſtminſter Bridge Road, near what is now the approach to Waterloo Station. The notice in the *Public Advertiser* ſtates that the programme would include the following:

At the End of the third Aĉt, a very favourite Chorus in ACIS and GALATEA: Oh the Pleasures of the Plains, &c. End of Aĉt Four, The Song and Chorus in ALEXANDER'S FEAST: Happy Pair &c. To conclude with the Coronation Anthem, God save the King &c. In the course of the Evening's Entertainments, the celebrated and aſtonishing Maſter MOZART, lately arrived, a Child of 7 Years of Age, will perform several fine seleĉt Pieces of his own Composition on the Harpsichord and on the Organ, which has already given the higheſt Pleasure, Delight, and Surpriẓe to the greateſt Judges of Music in England or Italy and is juſtly eſteemed the moſt extraordinary Prodigy, and moſt amaẓing Genius that has appeared in any Age.[7]

Mozart presumably again played some of his Paris sonatas, but it is not clear what else he may have chosen for the organ. The programme, however, again emphasises the continued popularity of Handel's music for a fashionable audience. Leopold would not have received any remuneration for the charity concert, but in a letter referring to the event, he declares his motive for allowing his son to perform:

I am letting Wolfgang play a concerto on the organ at this concert in order to perform thereby the aĉt of an English patriot who, as far as in him lies, endeavours to further the usefulness of this hospital which has been eſtablished pro bono publico. That is, you see, one way of winning the affection of this quite exceptional nation.[8]

Leopold resolved that as the time was not propitious for arranging financially successful concerts in London, he would follow the nobility and gentry to Tunbridge Wells, one of their summer resorts within easy reach of London, where they took the waters. But it was not to be. On 8th July he was taken ill with a severe throat infection—what he called the native complaint of a 'cold'. Elaborating on this malady, he goes on to say that for this reason in England you hardly ever see people wearing summer clothes and they all wear cloth garments. The 'cold' could become dangerous and the wisest course was to flee the country![9] In fact, Leopold appears to have suffered a chill after hurrying to a concert to which he and his children had been invited by the Earl of Thanet at his house in Grosvenor Square. The exact nature of the subsequent illness is not clear, but it evidently laid him low for a month. In order for him to regain his health, the family moved from central London to the country village of Chelsea, about two miles distant, where they took lodgings in the house of a Mr George Randal and his family in Five Fields Row (now 180 Ebury Street). Leopold says, in a letter, that from the house he has one of the most beautiful views in the world. "Wherever I turn my eyes, I only see gardens and in the distance the finest castles; and the house in which I am living has a lovely garden".[10] They remained in Chelsea for seven weeks during which time no concerts could be arranged; financially, the episode was disastrous.

On 25th September, the family moved back to London and took up residence at the house of Mr Thomas Williamson, a corset maker, in Thrift Street (now 21 Frith Street), Soho. Leopold, fully recovered, was most anxious to retrieve some of his losses. A letter from Melchior Grimm in Paris, attempting to intervene on the Mozarts' behalf through the Duke of York, reveals that Leopold wished to hold a series of subscription concerts at the fashionable musical assemblies given by Mrs Theresa Cornelys in Soho.[11] But, there is no documentary evidence that the Mozart children ever performed there and it is seems that the plan came to nought.

A further blow to Leopold's plans to woo the aristocracy was dealt to him when he learnt that, contrary to the usual custom, the king had delayed the summoning of Parliament for two months until 10 January, which meant that the nobility remained out of town, "and therefore guineas are not yet flying about and I am still living on my purse". However, a slight solace to him was an invitation for the children to perform at Buckingham House on the evening of 25th October, the anniversary of the king's accession to the throne. This was the last occasion that they appeared at court and no details of the performance are given apart from the fact it lasted for four hours.

Their next public concert was originally arranged for 15th February 1765, but owing to a performance of Arne's oratorio *Judith* on that date it did not take place until Thursday, 21st February, when "the prodigies of nature", their ages again trimmed by one year, were advertised to appear at the Little Theatre, Haymarket, in a benefit concert of vocal and instrumental music to begin exactly at six, "which will not hinder the nobility and gentry from meeting in other assemblies on the same evening".[12] This is, perhaps, a reference to an entertainment held by Mrs Theresa Cornelys every Thursday at Carlisle House. It is stated that all the overtures (symphonies) would be from the composition of these "astonishing composers" [sic]. These could have been the symphonies, K.16 and K.19, and possibly K³.19a, the first of which Mozart wrote during his stay in Chelsea the previous summer. Copies of the manuscripts were made by Leopold himself to save the cost of one shilling for each sheet. The price of admission was again half a guinea, and he made a profit of about one hundred guineas.

By then Leopold was getting a little disgruntled about the London musical scene, saying that on account of the number of entertainments, "which really weary one here", the concert was not so well attended as he had hoped. He then goes on to make the cryptic statement that he knew why they were not being more generously treated in London. This was because he had not accepted a certain proposal made to him

a matter upon which I have decided deliberately after mature consideration and several sleepless nights and which is now done with, as I will not bring up my children in such a dangerous place (where the majority of the inhabitants have no religion and where one only has evil examples before one).[13]

The nature of the offer made, or by whom, is not disclosed but it presumably meant that a long-term contract would have been given to the Mozart children. It was apparently turned down by their father on social rather than financial grounds.

There is now a feeling that the novelty value of the Mozart children was waning and that their financial worth was on the decline. By March

Leopold was of the opinion that the time had come to leave England. Advertisements were circulated for a final concert to be given at Hickford's Great Room. He was now desperate to attract an audience and there were notable differences in the tone of the advertisements. The price of admission was reduced to five shillings and, as an added inducement to buy tickets, the public were invited to visit the Mozarts' house in Thrift Street and to put the children's abilities to the test at home every day from twelve until two o'clock. Here the book of Wolfgang's sonatas was also on sale at half a guinea and even prints of the watercolour, originally painted in Paris by the artist, Louis de Carmontelle, depicting the children performing with their father, were offered for two shillings and sixpence.[14] The concert did not in fact take place until 13th May, and the accompanying soloists again included Clementina Cremonini and Francois Barthélemon, as in their first public performance almost a year earlier. The works included Wolfgang's London symphonies as well as a new harpsichord concerto for four hands, possibly K³.19d. The performance was notable for the fact that the children used the new two-manual harpsichord built for King Frederick II of Prussia by the well-known maker Burkhart Shudi, whom Leopold knew. A letter in the Salzburg *Europaeische Zeitung* of 6th August 1765, probably inspired by Leopold, states

Mr Thudy has moreover conceived the good notion of having his extraordinary instrument played for the first time by the most extraordinary clavier player in this world, namely by the very celebrated master of music Wolfg. Mozart, aged nine, the admirable son of the Salzburg Kapellmeister, Herr L. Mozart. It was quite enchanting to hear the fourteen-year-old sister of this little virtuoso playing the most difficult sonatas on the clavier with the most astonishing dexterity and her brother accompanying her extempore on another clavier. Both perform wonders.[15]

Leopold makes no reference to the outcome of this final concert, but it does not seem to have been a great financial success since he was driven to further expediencies to raise money. Gone were the high principles surrounding the early performance for charity before the fashionable audience of Ranelagh. He was reduced to inserting the following advertisement in the *Public Advertiser* of 8th July:

Mr MOZART the Father of the celebrated young Musical family, who have so

justly raised the Admiration of the greatest Musicians in Europe, has been obliged by the Desire of several Ladies and Gentlemen to postpone his Departure from England for a short Time, takes this Opportunity to inform the Public that he has taken the great Room in the Swan and Harp Tavern in Cornhill, where he will give an Opportunity to all the Curious to hear these two young Prodigies perform every Day from Twelve to Three. Admittance 2s 6d each Person.[16]

A subsequent notice stated that "The Two Children will also play together with four Hands upon the same Harpsichord and put upon it a Handkerchief without seeing the Keys."

The circumstances of these last public performances of the Mozart children before they left London on 24th July sound more like a circus act than a serious contribution to music. However, before their departure, an important independent witness of Wolfgang's precocious talent as a performer and as a composer appeared in the person of the Honourable Daines Barrington, an eminent lawyer, a friend of the naturalist Gilbert White of Selborne and Fellow of the Royal Society.

Daines Barrington was also an amateur musician. Having attended public concerts at which Wolfgang had performed, he was so intrigued by what he had heard that he was determined to put the abilities of this apparent prodigy to proper tests. In June he visited the Mozart house in Thrift Street and spent a considerable time alone with the boy. He subsequently provided a detailed report of his findings, which was read at a meeting of the Royal Society and then published in their proceedings.[17] The assessment was very thorough. Barrington states:

I carried to him a manuscript duet, which was composed by an English gentleman to some favourite words in Metastasio's opera of Demofoonte. The whole score was in five parts, viz. accompaniments for a first and second violin, two vocal parts, and a base. . . . My intention in carrying with me this manuscript composition, was to have an irrefragable proof of his abilities, as a player at sight, it being absolutely impossible that he could have ever seen the music before. The score was no sooner put upon his desk than he began to play the symphony in a most masterly manner, as well as in the time and stile which corresponded with the intention of the composer. . . . The symphony ended, he took the upper part, leaving the under one to his father. His voice in the tone of it was thin and infantine, but nothing could exceed the masterly manner in which he sung. His father, who took the under part in the duet, was once or twice out, though the passages were not more difficult than those in the upper one; on which occasions the son looked back with some anger pointing out to him his mistakes, and setting him right. He not only however did complete justice to the duet, by singing his own part in the truest taste, and with the greatest precision: he also threw in the accompaniments of the two violins, wherever they were most necessary, and produced the best effects.

Daines Barrington goes on to explain how very difficult it is for even experienced musicians to read at sight two violin parts, the voice part, the words and the bass all simultaneously. His account casts an interesting light on the professional relationship between father and son. At the age of nine Wolfgang had become, musically, the master of Leopold.

Barrington then wished to test Wolfgang's abilities as a composer.

Happening to know that the little Mozart was much taken notice of by Manzoli, the famous singer, who came over to England in 1764, I said to the boy, that I should be glad to hear an extemporary Love Song such as his friend Manzoli might choose in an opera. The boy on this (who continued to sit at his harpsichord) looked back with much archness, and immediately began five or six lines of a jargon recitative proper to introduce a love song.

He then played a symphony which might correspond with an air composed to the single word, Affetto. It had a first and second part, which, together with the symphonies was of the length that opera songs generally last. . . . Finding that he was in humour, and as it were inspired, I then desired him to compose a Song of Rage, such as might be proper for the opera stage. The boy again looked back with much archness, and began five or six lines of a jargon recitative proper to precede a Song of Anger. This lasted also about the same time with the Song of Love; and in the middle of it he had worked himself up to such a pitch that he beat his harpsichord like a person possessed, rising sometimes in his chair. The word he pitched upon for this second extemporary composition was, Perfido. After this he played a difficult lesson, which he had finished a day or two before: his execution was amazing, considering that his little fingers could scarcely reach a fifth on the harpsichord.

His astonishing readiness, however, did not arise merely from great practice; he had a thorough knowledge of the fundamental principles of composition, as, upon producing a treble, he immediately wrote a base under it, which, when tried, had a very good effect. . . . The facts which I have been mentioning I was

31

myself an eyewitness of; to which I must add that I have been informed by two or three able musicians, when Bach the celebrated composer had begun a fugue and left off abruptly, that little Mozart hath immediately taken it up and worked it after a most masterly manner.

Taking nothing for granted, Daines Barrington ends his report by saying that he had even checked up on the boy's true age by obtaining details from the register of births in Salzburg.

Here was irrefutable proof of Mozart's "extraordinary genius" when of almost "infantine" age.

❧ CHAPTER IV ❧
THE COMPOSITIONS IN LONDON

LEOPOLD WAS PARTICULARLY PROUD OF THE FACT THAT WHEN HE ADVERTISED concerts to be performed by his "prodigies of nature" they would play compositions written by Wolfgang himself. In all, there are twelve complete works in existence, as well as a collection of fragments, which Wolfgang is believed to have composed during the fifteen months that he was in London. There are others, including at least one symphony and probably some keyboard sonatas which have been lost.

The first indication of his London works came on 18th January 1765 when there appeared six sonatas for the harpsichord "which can be played with the accompaniment of the violin or transverse flute", engraved and printed at Leopold's own expense, and dedicated to "Her Majesty Charlotte, Queen of Great Britain". The six sonatas were sent to the queen accompanied by an extravagantly flowery letter, written in French by Leopold, but signed, "Your Majesty's very humble and obedient little servant, J. G. W. Mozart".[1] For these compositions Wolfgang received fifty guineas from the queen.

Because there were so many amateur players of music at that period, there was a ready market for small keyboard works with optional accompaniment. Trading on the royal connection, Leopold put the sonatas on general sale from 20th March for the price of half a guinea. In the copies presented by Leopold to the British Museum there is also an optional cello accompaniment.

These six sonatas, K.10–K.15, contain either two or three short movements. For the most part, they are undoubtedly inspired by the composers with whom Wolfgang had been in closest contact. The first and the fourth of the series, K.10 and K.13, show close similarities to the previous three sonatas written in Paris, under the influence of Johann Schobert, giving the impression that they were written earlier than the others. These works written for the keyboard and violin generally show little in the way of an independent role for the violin, and the cello, when played, simply reinforces the bass part. The most original pieces are to be found in the Andante movements of K.13 and K.15, where the violin asserts itself more obviously. These sonatas are essentially similar to those of many composers of the time, notably Schobert, Honauer and Eckard in Paris, as well as C. F. Abel and J. C. Bach in London. Nevertheless, they are still astonishing as the works of an eight-year-old.

In the late nineteenth century there emerged a notebook labelled, in Leopold's writing, "*di Wolfgango Mozart a Londra 1764*" in which were forty-three very short musical pieces in Wolfgang's hand. The first twenty-four are written in pencil and the remainder are in ink. Known as the London (Chelsea) notebook, K⁶.15a-ss, it was published in 1909 and consists of short sketches, mostly for the keyboard, but in a few cases there are indications of orchestration suggestive of drafts for a symphony. They were probably used by Mozart as the basis of some of his early works. Most of them were said to have been written during the family's stay in Chelsea. In recent times some have been arranged and orchestrated for performance.[2]

The Mozarts were in Chelsea from July to September 1764, when Leopold was convalescing from his severe illness. Many years later, in January 1800, Mozart's sister Nannerl recalls this period in her memoirs:

In London, where our father lay dangerously ill, we were forbidden to touch a piano. So, to keep himself occupied, Mozart composed his first symphony for all the instruments of the orchestra, but in particular, for the trumpets and kettledrums. I sat down at his side and copied it out. As he composed and I copied he said,—'Remind me to give the horn something worthwhile to do!'"[3]

Traditionally, this first symphony, composed in Chelsea in 1764, is the one in E flat major, K.16. There are, however, difficulties in reconciling this work with Nannerl's statement. Firstly, K.16 contains no parts for the trumpet or kettledrum and, secondly, there is no special provision for the horns. Either Nannerl was referring to yet another symphony, now lost, or, quite possibly, after a lapse of thirty five years her memory was at fault.

At that point in the eighteenth century, the symphony took a different form from that which developed later in Mozart's life. It was often referred to as an overture, because it was similar to the short orchestral work which preceded a main feature, whether it be a play, opera or concert. The symphony, written in the new galant style, had been introduced into England by a Scot, Thomas Alexander Erskine, sixth Earl of Kellie. He had spent nearly three years in Mannheim, where he had played the violin, and on his return in 1756 he published six symphonies closely similar to those composed by Johann Stamitz for his famous orchestra. They were short, in three movements, written in the Mannheim style with its crescendo and diminuendo and sudden contrasts between forte and piano. A few years later, with the arrival of C. F. Abel and J. C. Bach, the more Italianate galant symphony appeared. But there were many other composers producing symphonies during the time Mozart was in London. Thomas Arne, in particular, embraced the new style, as well as William Bates, George Rush, Francois Barthélemon and Felice Giardini.

Whatever the exact time of its composition, K.16 is the earliest Mozart symphony in existence. Like others of the time, it is in three short movements and is scored for two oboes, two horns and strings. The first movement, Allegro, begins with a loud fanfare followed by the favourite J. C. Bach device of a contrasting piano phrase. The very short Andante, a binary movement in C minor, has the oboes setting the scene, and the final Presto begins with another fanfare ending with a light brilliant rondo. The whole work is very evocative of the Italianate style of J. C. Bach with touches derived from Abel.

Indeed, as testimony of Abel's early influence, the so-called Symphony No. 3, K.18, for many years regarded as Mozart's work, was later shown to be a perfect copy of a work by Abel (Symphony No. 6, Op. 7). It was made by Mozart before it had appeared in published form, and he probably saw the manuscript through the intercession of his father after he had heard it at one of the Bach-Abel concerts early in 1765. Symphony No. 2, K.17, is now recognised to be a work entirely by Leopold.

The next authentic symphony is that in D major, K.19, and, like K.16, it is scored for pairs of oboes and horns with strings but it already shows advances on its predecessor. It opens in a similar manner with a forte fanfare followed by a piano phrase but it is more brilliant. There is an individual Mozartian touch in the sudden A sharp which begins the second half of this Allegro movement. The G major Andante has only two horns and strings and is very much in the style of J. C. Bach's Opus 3 symphonies of 1765. The final 3/8 Presto is in the form of a spirited jig.

There is reason to believe from Leopold's writing and from the catalogue of the music publishers, Breitkopf and Hartel, that Mozart composed four symphonies during his stay in London, but only three can now be confidently ascribed to him. The third reappeared as recently as 1981 and was inscribed in Leopold's hand "Sinfonia in F / a 2 violinj / 2 hautb: / 2 cornj / viola / e / basso / di Wolfgango Mozart / compositore de 9 Anj." This symphony, K³.19a, was, like K.19, probably written early in 1765 for the concert given by Wolfgang on 21st February, since Leopold states that *all* the overtures (symphonies) at this performance were by Wolfgang. The symphony in F major is of similar quality to K.19. Like that of K.19, the first movement, Allegro assai, is in binary form but is otherwise superior to the earlier work, and it contains brief passages of imitative writing. The B flat Andante is very expressive, with the violins and viola dominating, the oboes being silent, and then follows a 3/8 Presto with a lively rondo as the finale. All three symphonies show that even at the tender age of eight or nine, Mozart was already conversant with the fashionable galant style of the time.

The last public performance of the Mozart children in London was on 13th May 1765 in Hickford's Great Room, Brewer Street. The announcement of this concert in the *Public Advertiser* includes the statement that there would be performed a "concerto on the harpsichord by the little composer and his sister, each singly and both together."[4] In the biography of Mozart by Constanze's second husband G. N. Nissen, a letter from Leopold is quoted as saying "Wolfgang composed his first piece for four hands in London. No such four-hand sonata had ever been composed before that time".[5] Whether Leopold wrote such a statement is doubtful since it does not appear in the original manuscript of the letter and the information may have been given to Nissen later by Nannerl. The work referred to in the public announcement is considered by some, but not all, to be the Sonata for Four Hands in C major, K³.19d. In a letter to Breitkopf and Hartel, in 1800, Nannerl hints that there were other such sonatas, in which case they are now lost.[6] If this sonata dates from 1765, it is an extraordinarily assured work for a nine-year-old; the middle movement of Menuetto and Trio is particularly fine. An interesting point about its performance is that the final rondo necessitates the crossing of the right hand of the lower register player, with the left hand playing the higher register, and this moment is seen in the well-known family portrait, painted about 1780, of Wolfgang and Nannerl playing a duet at the keyboard.

The remaining two works which were written in London are vocal compositions. It is already very apparent how Mozart was affected by J. C. Bach in his instrumental works, but another influential figure in Mozart's musical education in London was the famous castrato singer Manzuoli. From him Wolfgang assimilated the operatic technique which was to amaze the Honourable Daines Barrington when the young boy was asked to compose extempore a "Song of Rage" and a "Song of Love". Wolfgang would have heard Manzuoli in the pasticcio opera *Ezio*, performed at the King's Theatre in November 1764. Some time after this date he wrote his first aria 'Va, dal furor portata', K.21, with a text from *Ezio* by Metastasio. It is a typical 'rage' aria of the time and was written not for Manzuoli but for the tenor, Ercole Ciprandi, who sang the secondo role of the father in the opera. The aria is particularly elaborate in its orchestration for oboes, bassoons, horns and strings, and may have been intended for a concert performance.

Finally, to demonstrate his son's virtuosity as a composer to the London musical establishment, Leopold arranged for Wolfgang to write a four part vocal work, 'God is our Refuge', K.20, which he presented to the British Museum shortly before their departure from London. It is a setting of the first verse of Psalm 46 and displays a polyphonic character which is an amazing example of the boy's precocity. The music is entirely in Wolfgang's hand, as is the first part of the text (towards the end of the first line where he misjudged the space available for the words the writing is taken over by Leopold). The manuscript is still in the possession of the British Museum and is the only example of a Mozart text written by him in English.

The London works composed when Mozart was between eight and nine display, not surprisingly, unmistakable signs of naivety. The instrumental pieces are highly derivative, particularly of J. C. Bach, but, written at this tender age, they are truly astounding, and the later works already contain enough shafts of brilliant innovation to portend the greatness to come.

FIG. 3. Johann Christian Bach (1735–82). Painting by Thomas Gainsborough, 1776.
By courtesy of the National Portrait Gallery, London.

THE INFLUENCE OF J. C. BACH

THROUGHOUT THEIR TRAVELS, LEOPOLD MOZART WAS CAREFUL TO ENSURE that his son met the most important musicians of the time. It was his son's unfailing ability to assimilate their various techniques which gave young Mozart such an unrivalled education. A few weeks after their arrival in London, Leopold was able to write, "what he knew when we left Salzburg is a mere shadow compared with what he knows now . . . in a word, my boy knows, in this his eighth year, what one would expect only from a man of forty."[1]

The two composers who dominated the concert scene in London were Carl Friedrich Abel and Johann Christian Bach. Abel, perhaps because of his greater affinity with the Germanic Leopold, was early brought to Wolfgang's attention but it was not long before he came under the spell of Bach. A little over a month after they came to London, Leopold wrote of his son to his friend Lorenz Hagenauer in Salzburg, "He greets you from the clavier, where at the moment he is seated, playing through Kapellmeister Bach's trio".[2]

Born in Leipzig on 5th September 1735, Johann Christian Bach was the youngest son of Johann Sebastian by his second marriage. After his father's death in 1750, Christian came under the tutelage of his elder half-brother, Carl Philipp Emanuel, in Berlin, where he excelled as a performer at the harpsichord and began his own compositions for the keyboard in the manner of Carl Philipp Emanuel. However, it was at the court of Frederick the Great, his brother's employer, that the younger Bach became acquainted for the first time with Italian opera, an experience which was to change his life completely. Until now he had been under the Germanic influence of his great father and, more recently, his brother, but now it was Italian music that fired his imagination.

In 1754 he left Berlin for Milan, where he was able to obtain employment as musician in the service of a prominent nobleman, Chevalier Count Agostino Litta. Very soon he obtained leave from his employer to study in Bologna with the maestro di cappella of San Francesco, Padre Martini, who, fourteen years later, was to receive the young Mozart. By

January 1757 he was in Naples, renowned for its schools of music and the San Carlo opera. He returned to Milan three months later and spent the next five years there, but only intermittently. During this time he wrote prolifically, including much liturgical music, with the benign approval of Padre Martini, but also chamber music and opera. In all he wrote three operas which were produced with great success, the first of which was *Artaserse*, performed in Turin in 1760.[3] There followed *Catone in Utica* (1761) and, two months later, *Alessandro nell'Indie*, both for the San Carlo opera in Naples.

By this time Johann Christian had become much more highly regarded in Italy and the rest of Europe than his father, who was virtually unknown outside his native Germany. He was now thoroughly Italianate, so much so that, eschewing his strict Lutheran upbringing, he was received into the Catholic Church. This paved the way for his appointment, in 1760, to the position of organist at Milan cathedral.

However, he was not to remain in post for very long. His fame as a lyric composer had spread and in 1762 Bach received an invitation from the English court. He arrived in London during the summer of that year. He soon became involved in its exciting musical life, and early in 1763 he was appointed music master to the queen. In addition to his duties at court, both as composer and teacher, Bach was engaged by the King's Theatre to write Italian opera. Here he began by providing contributions to the pasticcio operas, but in February 1763 he produced *Orione*, his first complete opera in England, to great acclaim. This was followed in May by his second opera, *Zanaida*, which was again a great success. In the meantime he was busy with instrumental compositions and in February 1764, in conjunction with his compatriot Abel, he began a series of concerts which were to continue for nearly twenty years.

Two months later the Mozart family arrived and Wolfgang quickly became acquainted with the music of the 'English' Bach. The early appearance of the Mozart children at court would have been arranged by Bach, who was obviously greatly taken by little Wolfgang. There is a report by Melchior Grimm, in his Parisian publication *Correspondance Littéraire*, that when in London, Wolfgang played before the king and queen sitting on Bach's lap, and that they played alternately on the same keyboard for two hours together, extempore.[4]

The musician and composer William Jackson of Exeter recalled another occasion:

John Bach took the child between his knees and began a subject (on the harpsichord) which he left, and Mozart continued—each led the other into very abstruse harmonies, and extraneous modulations, in which child beat the man. We were afterwards looking over Bach's famous song 'Se spiego' in 'Zanaida'. The score was inverted to Mozart, who was rolling on the table. He pointed out a note which he said was wrong. It was so, whether of the composer or copyist I cannot now recollect, but it was an instance of extraordinary discernment and readiness in a mere infant.[5]

Johann Christian Bach wrote in the Italianate, so-called galant style, a term originally used in the eighteenth century to denote the new generation of music, graceful, courtly, and uncomplicated, and written largely in a homophonic manner, in strong contradistinction to the contrapuntal compositions of J. S. Bach and his contemporaries. Later, 'galant' took on a more pejorative meaning, being regarded as facile, lacking in depth, and it is only more recently that J. C. Bach has been given his proper due. To the thin Italian style he brought a strengthening and richer texture occasioned by his Germanic upbringing. It is his sense of melody and elegance, together with a mastery of orchestration, which proved to be so congenial to the young Mozart. His compositions provided the basis of much of the boy's early work in London, as already described. Bach's own youthful conversion from the German baroque to the Neopolitan style was instinctively seized upon by his young admirer, who, a few years later was, like Bach, to experience the delights of Italy for himself. In the meantime, Wolfgang was happy to shake off the influence of his own austere Germanic father for the lighter aspect of Johann Christian Bach. During this time Bach was living in a joint bachelor establishment with Abel in King's Court, adjoining Soho Square, a very fashionable area, and close to Mrs Cornelys' Carlisle Rooms. In January 1765 the Bach-Abel subscription concerts were transferred there; it is clear from Leopold Mozart's mention of Mrs Cornelys in his notebook that they attended these performances. At these concerts Bach's and Abel's own compositions predominated and here Wolfgang would have been able to experience their instrumental technique.

It seems likely that J. C. Bach , in 1768, was one of the first in England to play the piano at a public performance. The fortepiano, as it was then called, was developed in London in the 1760s by the maker Johann Zumpe, with whom Leopold Mozart became acquainted. Bach was early attracted to the new instrument, since unlike the harpsichord, it had the ability to be played loud or soft by touch, and its superior expressive range lent itself to the nature of his music. As early as 1766 Bach had advertised six of his sonatas, Op. 5, as being written "for the harpsichord or fortepiano" and by the late 1770s he was performing exclusively on the piano.[6] Contemporary accounts emphasise the easygoing manner of Bach's disposition, his elegant charm and his ready smile, characteristics which endeared him to his young protégé. In 1776 Padre Martini invited Bach, his former pupil, to provide a portrait of himself for the gallery of musicians he was forming in Bologna. Bach chose Thomas Gainsborough, with whom he had been friendly for several years, to be the artist and the resulting portrait, which is still in Bologna, completely captures the kindly expression of the composer. Gainsborough subsequently painted a copy for Bach himself, which is now in the National Portrait Gallery.

Bach's influence can be seen long after Mozart's departure from England. In 1772, as an example of his early attempts to master the concerto, Wolfgang selected three of Bach's sonatas, Nos. 2, 3 and 4, Op. 5 and converted them into clavier concertos, K.107, 1–3, by adding orchestration. These were used by him not only as exercises but to perform at concerts.

In Mozart's compositions for the keyboard, numerous elements of Bach continue to be encountered. Thus, for example, the opening Allegro movement of the Piano Sonata in B flat, K.333, is strongly reminiscent of Bach's Sonata No. 4 in G, Op. 17, which Bach may have shown Mozart when they met in 1778; and in the slow movement of the Piano Concerto in A major, K.414, of 1782, Mozart uses music from Bach's lovely overture to the London revival of the pasticio opera *La calamita de cuori*. In 1784 Mozart took a theme from the opening movement of one of Bach's best-known piano concertos, No. 4, Op. 13, for his own Piano Concerto in B flat, K.456. Even as late as 1786, Mozart's Rondo in D major, K.485, incorporates a theme taken from Bach's Quintet in No. 6 in D, Op. 11. Written between 1772 and 1777, these quintets are some of the finest examples of Bach's chamber music.

In the field of opera the two figures present during the 1764–65 London season who were a particular inspiration to the young boy were the singer Giovanni Manzuoli and J. C. Bach. Together they helped to form his extraordinarily precocious knowledge of the art of opera. In November, an aria which Bach provided for the pasticcio *Ezio* so impressed Mozart that years later, in 1778, he wrote,

For practice I have also set to music the aria 'Non so d'onde viene' etc. which has

been so beautifully composed by Bach. Just because I know Bach's setting so well and like it so much, and because it is always ringing in my ears, I wished to try and see whether in spite of all this I could not write an aria totally unlike his.[7]

Apart from the contributions to other pasticcios, he would also have heard Bach's full-length opera *Adriano in Sirio*. Five years after he had left England, Mozart also came to Milan to write his first opera in Italy, *Mitridate, re di Ponto*. By this time he was fully versed in the opera seria style of Bach. For his second operatic work for Milan, *Ascanio in Alba*, he wrote the main role for the same castrato as Bach had composed for in London, the great Manzuoli. As C. S. Terry, Bach's biographer, says, "In the domain of opera Bach's elegance, melodic purity, inclination to subordinate dramatic expression to sheer beauty of phrase, were characteristics he imparted to his young disciple, who added the qualities of his own flaming genius".[8] It was in his later operas, when he added intense dramatic expression to the exquisite beauty of his music, that Mozart rose to heights that Bach, fixed in the mould of opera seria, could never hope to achieve.

In 1773 Bach left the house he had shared with Abel in Soho to marry the operatic soprano Cecilia Grassi, but he continued to take part in their joint concerts, as well as to compose instrumental music and songs, especially for the audiences at Vauxhall. His operatic works became fewer and he was to write only two more operas for the English stage, *Carattaco* in 1767 and then, after a long interval, *La clemenza di Scipione* in 1778. Both were reasonable successes but it is clear that by now Bach had begun to lose favour with the King's Theatre management, who were casting around for fresh composers.

Bach continued to write for theatres abroad and in August 1778 he arrived in Paris to prepare his opera *Amadis de Gaule*. It was here that he met Mozart again after an interval of thirteen years. The depth of feeling that Bach had engendered in him as a boy had never been lost and is graphically described by Mozart in a letter to his father, written after being reunited with his old mentor. He had come to Paris from Mannheim in the company of his mother, five months previously, looking for employment. But it was a disastrous period for him. Not only did the commissions not materialise, but one month before he met Bach he had witnessed the death of his beloved mother from fever at their lodgings in Paris. He wrote to his father in Salzburg:

Mr Bach from London has been here for the last fortnight. He is going to write a

*French opera, and has only come to hear the singers. He will then go back to
London and compose the opera, after which he will return here to see it staged.
You can easily imagine his delight and mine at meeting again; perhaps his delight may not have been quite as sincere as mine—but one must admit that he is
an honourable man and willing to do justice to others. I love him (as you know)
and respect him with all my heart; and as for him, there is no doubt but that he
has praised me warmly, not only to my face, but to others also, and in all seri-
ousness—not in the exaggerated manner which some affect.*[9]

This expression of Mozart's feelings is particularly remarkable when it is
realised that in his more mature years he had developed a low opinion of
most of his fellow composers, treating many of them with contempt or
suspicion; the love that he had for Bach was matched only by that he felt
for Haydn.

Bach never saw Mozart again after his return to London. The Bach-
Abel concerts continued, now at the new concert room in Hanover Square.
Bach was still a great favourite at court, and he and his wife were frequent
performers at musical parties attended by the Prince of Wales and other
notables, including the painter Zoffany. But his music had lost its appeal
with the wider audiences, so that attendances at the subscription concerts
fell, and his extravagant lifestyle, together with his falling musical output,
led to a marked decline in his financial state. Nevertheless, his late symphonies, Op. 18, published in 1781, are some of his best orchestral works.
Three of these are scored for two orchestras and are particularly fine examples of inspired instrumentation, the first orchestra providing a magnificent contrast to the second. But by now his health had begun to
deteriorate seriously and in May 1781 he gave his last performance at the
Hanover Square Rooms. By the end of the year it was obvious that he
would not recover, and a great friend, Charlotte Papendiek, lady-in-
waiting to the queen, visited him with her husband-to-be and her parents.
In her memoirs, written many years later, she remarks, "The last visit we
paid was together with my father and mother. Bach, on taking a final leave
joined our hands. I think now I see his enchanting smile. Not a word was
said; we were motionless".[10] On 1st January 1782 Johann Christian Bach
died at the age of forty-six, leaving debts amounting to £4000. He was
buried in St Pancras's churchyard in the presence of only four friends. The
queen paid for his funeral and gave financial assistance to his widow, but
such is the fickleness of public esteem that towards the end of his life his

musical reputation had shrunk to the extent that his death occurred without any official comment being made. Charlotte Papendiek says sadly, "This man of ability in his profession, of liberal kindness in it, of general attention to friends, and of worthy character, was forgotten almost before he was called to the doom of us all, and every recollection of him seems buried in oblivion".[11] One person, however, did not forget. Mozart, writing to his father from Vienna, on 10th April 1782 said "I suppose you have heard that the English Bach is dead? What a loss to the musical world!"[12]

After nearly a century and a half of neglect, C. S. Terry's detailed biography of the 'English' Bach was published. Since then, increased interest in eighteenth-century music in England has led to renewed attention being given to a composer who had such a profound influence on Mozart during his formative years. This interest is not just confined to scholars, as the gramophone record and compact disc have now enabled many to appreciate this master of the galant, with his marvellous sense of melody, colour and charm. It is now realised that while he may have been eclipsed by his illustrious protégé and other famous composers of the classical period, Johann Christian Bach nevertheless composed a great amount of fine music—fine enough to inspire the little genius from Salzburg.

FIG. 4. Manuscript page of four part vocal work 'God is our refuge', K.20. Words written by Wolfgang with the help of his father Leopold Mozart, and presented by Leopold Mozart to the British Museum (see page 53 below). *By Permission of the British Library: Music Library, K.10.a.17.(3).*

✤ CHAPTER VI ✤

MOZART FAMILY LIFE IN LONDON

AS THE MOZART FAMILY ENTERED LONDON ON A LATE SPRING DAY IN 1764, they drove through the congested, filthy streets of the city, teeming with pedestrians, carriages, wagons, carts and livestock going to market, before proceeding to Piccadilly where they spent the first night at The White Bear Inn. The following day they moved to lodgings at the house of a barber, Mr John Couzin, of 19 Cecil Court, St Martin's Lane. Leopold Mozart states that they had three small rooms, for which they paid twelve shillings a week. The rooms were smaller than they wished, but they were in Westminster, where the Court, much of the nobility, and the theatres, all of which Leopold regarded as of great importance, were situated.

In his long letters to Lorenz Hagenauer in Salzburg, he reported the many aspects of life in London which struck him as being so different from Paris and certainly from provincial Salzburg.[1] The very size of the city was overwhelming. He noted its cosmopolitan nature; many foreign nationalities, including Portuguese, Spanish, Italians, Germans and Sephardic Jews, who had settled in London for over a century, but all tending to segregate into separate localities. The area where the Mozart family lived had benefitted from the recent Westminster Paving Acts of 1761, which, for the first time, provided for the paving and lighting of the streets by the parish authorities. Leopold marvelled at the lavish scale of the illumination in this part of London which burned all night, and he remarked upon the size of some of the rich houses, the well laid out streets and the large squares adorned by statues of the king and other dignitaries. In contrast, he noted the maze of small courts and alleys to the east where the less fortunate lived. "Here it is hard for the poor," he says, "although very few beg openly, because it is forbidden by law, but many are in the streets selling flowers, matches, ribbons, or they sing songs and sell their ballads".[2]

The daily diet of the family is recorded. In the morning they drank strong tea with a little milk or cream and ate bread and butter, sometimes toasted. The next meal was taken at two o'clock consisting of roast meat, either mutton or beef. In the evening they might have soup and preserved veal. The usual drink of the citizens was porter or other kinds of beer, but since this did not suit the Mozarts they drank Italian wine, diluted with water for which they paid two shillings a bottle. They saw the vast amount of food which was on display in the shops and markets of Smithfield, Covent Garden and Billingsgate. Here was fish of all kinds, including oysters, which Leopold says were very cheap, the largest costing four pennies for a dozen. He says that he stood on London Bridge and looked across at the forest of masts of the ships lying in the Thames as far distant as the Tower awaiting the discharge of their cargoes brought from all over the world.

Leopold found the English weather very uncongenial, particularly in winter, when the dark, damp fogs and smoke of London were most unhealthy, so that they all developed colds. But in summer, the whole family delighted in strolling in St James's Park or Green Park in the company of other Londoners.

One of the highlights of their leisure activity was to visit the pleasure gardens. Like many other observers in the eighteenth century, Leopold thought Vauxhall was astonishing with its brilliantly illuminated avenues, thousands of lights arranged in arches and pyramids, and a central open pavilion with bandstand and organ. He noted the beautifully dressed women in their silk and taffeta, ribbons and pearls and yet he was impressed with the manner in which the nobility and the ordinary people mixed so freely at Vauxhall.[3] "Everything was enchanting; I did not know where to look first".[4]

Ranelagh Pleasure Gardens, although smaller, were also a great favourite. Here they could enter for two shillings and sixpence and obtain coffee or tea, bread and butter, as much as they could consume. The great Rotunda accommodated three thousand people and was heated in the cold weather by fires in the central support. Here, Leopold says, the music of the main concert would last from seven o'clock until ten and then this would be followed by a quartet playing the horn, clarinets and bassoon for another hour or so.

The Mozart family spent their time in London not only in the pursuit of music but also in seeing the famous sights of the city. Leopold says they visited the Tower of London and there, in the menagerie, the roar of the lions greatly frightened Wolfgang.[5] Nannerl, his sister, adds that they also saw a young elephant, a camel, and "a donkey with coffee-coloured stripes" (a zebra).[6] She says that they visited St Paul's Cathedral, the Monument, Lincoln's Inn Fields, Somerset House, the Foundling Hospital, Greenwich, the Royal Gardens at Kew, the Royal Chelsea Hospital, and many other places.

But Leopold also saw the darker side of London life. He was witness to the fury of the much-feared London mob. In May 1765 he records that the silk workers of Spitalfields protested against the importation of cheap French silks, causing unemployment. A crowd of over four thousand people, bearing black banners, "wearing their untidy green aprons, just as they did at work", streamed past his residence, and by the next day, he says, it had swollen to fifteen thousand people, assembled at Charing Cross.[7] The crowds marched on Parliament where they hurled abuse at the lords entering the parliament building. Particular venom was directed at the Duke of Bedford, who had opposed the duty on French silk imports. Leopold was well acquainted with the duke, having met him the previous year in Paris where he had been British ambassador. The greatly swollen mob proceeded to Bedford House in Bloomsbury Square, with the intention of seizing the duke and looting his house. They succeeded in tearing down the front pillars before a troop of cavalry and foot soldiers arrived. Leopold says that many of the crowd were ridden down and badly beaten. The crowd was ordered to disperse and notices were posted stating that if as many as twelve people congregated together they would be arrested and hanged. Unrest continued for the next four weeks. Leopold was also appalled by the frequent street fights. He saw the injuries men would inflict on each other while punching and biting, and on one occasion he saw two blacksmith apprentices fighting with glowing hot brands.

On 26th January 1765 the case of the eccentric fifth Lord Byron, great uncle of the poet, came to his notice.[8] After drinking in a tavern, Lord Byron fought a duel with his cousin, Mr Chaworth, who was run through by the noble lord's sword and died the following day. Lord Byron fled to France and was found guilty of manslaughter, although he escaped sentence by the fact that he was a peer.

Another aspect of English life which upset Leopold was a widespread lack of religious belief. He, a devout Catholic, was saddened by the behaviour of those of the upper classes who, because there were no theatres open on Sunday, the Lord's Day, drove out of the city to their country estates until the day of prayer was past. Similarly, taking their example, many ordinary people also stayed away from the churches. It was this laxity which had spurred the evangelism of John and Charles Wesley, who promoted Methodism in England during the eighteenth century.

Much that Leopold saw impressed him greatly, but it would appear that experience of the disturbing aspects of life in London finally persuaded him not to take up the offer of a firm contract to stay and bring up his children in England.

In his letters to Lorenz Hagenauer, Leopold goes into great detail about his illness which necessitated the whole family moving to rural Chelsea.[9] He mentions the difficulty in obtaining the kind of medicines he was used to in Salzburg, but these minutiae are of interest only to students of eighteenth century medicine. Of the several London doctors he must have consulted only two are named. One was a Dr Felix Macdonough, a surgeon practising in Oxford Street, whom Leopold may have called upon for their periodic blood-letting, regarded by him as a necessary health precaution.[10] The other was a certain Mr Christian Bossenburg, described by Leopold as royal surgeon and oculist, who lived in a large house in fashionable Bury Street, St James's.[11] He appears to have been too grand a person to attend to their ordinary medical needs, and the family may have encountered him socially.

Leopold Mozart's travel notebook lists the large number of important persons whom he met while in London.[12] Many, not unnaturally, were musicians, including the composers J. C. Bach, C. F. Abel, Thomas Arne, and George Rush as well as opera singers, instrumentalists of all kinds and harpsichord makers. He also met the portrait painter, Johann Zoffany (1733–1810) and the less well-known artist George James (d. 1795), a close neighbour in Dean Street, Soho, both of whom at that time exhibited at the Incorporated Society of Artists (the Royal Academy was not established until 1768). It has been suggested that a portrait of a boy with a bird's nest painted by Zoffany, now in the Mozarteum, Salzburg, is that of the young Wolfgang, but the identification is doubtful.[13] Whether they met the founder of the Royal Academy, Joshua Reynolds, is uncertain; although there is an entry note mentioning a Mr Reynous, of Little Mortimer Street near the Middlesex Hospital, Reynolds was, at that time, actually living in Leicester Fields (Leicester Square). One person of his circle whom Leopold apparently did not encounter was Dr Samuel Johnson, but then, the Great Cham of literature was said to be antipathetic to musicians. He once asked Charles Burney, "Pray sir, who is Bach? Is he a piper?"[14]

It is the list of foreign ambassadors and members of the aristocracy which proclaims Leopold's need to cultivate this class of society for their support in London, for private and public concerts, and to provide the necessary introductions for his future enterprises when he had left England. For example, he took care to meet Elizabeth, Duchess of Hamilton (1733–90), widow of the sixth duke, who was, like another acquaintance, Lady

Effingham, a Lady of the Bedchamber, with an entrée to Court. Similarly, he records a further member of the royal household, Mary, Duchess of Ancaſter (1730–93), whose musical intereſts may have prompted a performance at her house in Berkeley Square.

Among other prominent personages they met was Lady Margaret Clive (1733–1817), who also lived in Berkeley Square. She was the wife of the great Lord Clive of India. In a letter Leopold mentions a recent report in the newspapers of an important viſtory on 23rd Oſtober 1764 of Eaſt India Company troops over two Indian Nawabs, which had enabled Clive to consolidate his control of Bengal.[15] Lady Clive's husband had juſt returned to India to resume his governorship and, in a recently discovered letter to him written on 12th March 1765, Lady Clive refers to a concert which she planned to hold at her house the next day at which the great Manzuoli would sing and "the little Mozarts, the boy aged 8 and the girl 12 will also play moſt completely well".[16] It was ten years later that Lord Clive, overwhelmed by his efforts in India, came back to England and committed suicide in the house at 45 Berkeley Square where the Mozart children had performed.

Other members of the ariſtocracy included nineteen-year-old Lady Sophia Carteret (1746–71), who, in February 1765, as mentioned by Leopold, married the prominent Whig politician, Earl Shelburne (1737–1805) of Hill Street, Berkeley Square, and died at age twenty five. Leopold also records visiting a Lady Caroline Harrington (1722–84) and her "pretty family" of five daughters and two sons, who lived at Stable Yard, St James's. From his favourable impression it would appear that he was unaware of the reputation of Lady Harrington and her husband. Lord Harrington was then a lieutenant-general in the Guards who had fought with diſtinſtion at the battle of Fontenoy, but was regarded as a person of quite exceptional immorality. Caroline Harrington was one of the beauties of the time, but much given to wild ways, such as nurturing a notorious highwayman. A few years previously she had appeared at George III's coronation "covered with all the diamonds she could borrow, hire, or seize".[17] Mrs Mary Delaney, that chronicler of people of quality, writes, severely, that she gave up her whole life to vanity and folly, and Horace Walpole speaks of her in his letters as having a very bad charaſter.

An even more notorious person who appears in Leopold's notes is Miss Elizabeth Chudleigh (1720–88). He may have met her at Carlisle House since she was a friend of the impresario Theresa Cornelys. At the time Elizabeth Chudleigh was a maid of the Princess Auguſta, but was secretly married to the Honorable Augustus John Hervey, later Earl of Bristol. She was much given to holding lavish parties attended by the aristocracy, and at one masked ball she appeared in the character of Iphigenia but, according to Horace Walpole, she was "so naked that you would have taken her for Andromeda".[18] In 1769, while still the wife of Augustus Hervey, she married the Duke of Kingston. When her secret marriage finally emerged she was indicted for bigamy, but having now become the Countess of Bristol, she escaped sentence on the grounds that she was a peeress. Although generous to her friends — she assisted Mrs Cornelys in buying Carlisle House — she continued a life of dissipation in various European cities and died in Paris in 1788.

In July 1765, shortly before their departure from England, the Mozart family visited the British Museum. This great institution had been established thirteen years previously in Montagu House, Bloomsbury, and since 1759 it had been open to the public, but only for a restricted few. The Mozarts were thus favoured, and they may have been introduced by one of the trustees, a Fellow of the Royal Society, the Reverend Dr Thomas Birch (1705–66). In a letter of 9th July Leopold remarks on the serious fires which frequently occurred in London, and that while at dinner with a friend, the ambassador from Saxony, he learnt of a particularly devastating fire near the Thames, which had destroyed the stables of "my good friend Dr Birch" who, he says, lived in Norfolk Street, off the Strand. Leopold goes on to say that the family were met at the British Museum by another of the trustees, the Reverend Andrew Planta, Assistant Keeper of Printed Books, who was perhaps chosen to guide them round the exhibits because, being of Swiss origin, he spoke German.

The Museum had been established originally to house the great collection of art, antiquities and objects of natural history bequeathed by the physician Sir Hans Sloane (1660–1753) as well as the manuscript collections of Robert Harley, Earl of Oxford, and of Sir Robert Cotton. Nannerl mentions in her own diary that on this visit she saw the library, antiquities, all kinds of birds, fishes and small animals. But in spite of this impressive material, Leopold found the quality of the display to be lacking because, in 1770, when he was in Bologna with Wolfgang, he visited the Institute of Science in the Pallazzo Poggi. He said, "What I have seen in Bologna surpasses the British Museum. For here one can see not only the rarities of nature but everything that deserves the name of science, preserved like a dictionary in beautiful rooms and in a clean and orderly fashion."[19]

But the important tangible record of the Mozarts' visit is seen in the donations which Leopold made to the British Museum, and which remain to this day some of the treasures of the British Library.[20] The gift consisted of copies of Wolfgang's 'Paris' sonatas, K.6–K.9, and the 'London' sonatas dedicated to Queen Charlotte, K.10–15, an engraving of the watercolour of the Mozart family used by Leopold as a publicity piece, and, most valuable of all, the manuscript of the choral work 'God is Our Refuge', K.20, the text being written in English by young Wolfgang, assisted by his father.

The Secretary to the Trustees of the British Museum, Dr Mathew Maty, FRS, duly sent Leopold a receipt for the gifts, dated 19th July 1765,

Sir, I am ordered by the Standing Committee of the Trustees of the British Museum, to signify to You, that they have received the present of the musical performances of your very ingenious Son which You were pleased lately to make Them, and to return You their Thanks for the same.[21]

In spite of Leopold's reservations, he obviously found the visit memorable because he carefully retained this acknowledgement, which is now in the Mozarteum in Salzburg. Five days later the Mozarts left London, never to return.

On 24th July, they travelled to Bourne Place near Canterbury, Kent, where, according to Leopold, they stayed at the country home of an English gentleman, whom he refers to in his travel notes as Mr Horatio Mann Esqr, in order to see the Canterbury horse races. This person was Horace Mann (1744–1814), nephew of Sir Horace Mann, the British minister in Florence. It seems that in addition to attending the races, Leopold intended to arrange a concert for his children in Canterbury. A notice in the *Kentish Post* or *Canterbury News Letter* of 20th July 1765 states,

On Thursday, 25 July, at Eleven in the Forenoon, Will Be a Musical Performance, At the Town-Hall, in Canterbury, for the Benefit of Master Mozart, the celebrated German Boy, Aged eight years, and his Sister, Who have exhibited with universal Applause to the Nobility and Gentry in London. The Compositions and extempore Performances of this little Boy are the Astonishment of all Judges of Music. Admission 2s. 6d.[22]

However, there is no record from Leopold or any other source that this performance actually took place. One week later the family drove the short distance from Canterbury to Dover — "So I left England on August 1st, and sailed from Dover at ten in the morning."

Wolfgang departed as an accomplished musician. The previous fifteen months had provided a breadth of education which far surpassed anything to be obtained in any other European city, and he was to remember England for the rest of his life.

PART TWO
The English in Italy

FIG. 5. Thomas Linley (1756–78). Painting by Thomas Gainsborough. (See page 58 below.)
By Permission of the Trustees of the Dulwich Picture Gallery.

❧ CHAPTER VII ❧

FLORENCE

Thomas Linley

FOR MUCH OF THE EIGHTEENTH CENTURY, ITALY WAS THE DOMINANT country in Europe for the composition and performance of music. It was therefore natural that Leopold should wish his son to study at first hand the music of the country and to display his talent there. In all, father and son made three visits to Italy of which the first was the most extensive, lasting from December 1769 to March 1771. This was an exploratory tour, during which they visited many centres including Verona, Mantua, Venice, Bologna, Florence, Rome and Naples. During this period Wolfgang composed at least four symphonies, probably K.74, K.81, K.84, K.97, his first string quartet, K.80, as well as music for the keyboard and sacred music, culminating in his first opera for Milan, *Mitridate, re di Ponto*.

Wolfgang performed frequently at concerts, but in Italy these generally took place in the private houses of the nobility in the presence of small select audiences. It was during their tour of the major cities that Leopold and his son encountered many prominent Englishmen who, for a variety of reasons, thronged Italy at this time. Some, like Mozart, were fellow musicians; others were expatriates or were in the diplomatic service; and there were many who were carrying out the fashionable Grand Tour. The first of these meetings of consequence took place in the city so beloved of the English, Florence.

A journey from Bologna which took them across the Appenines in driving rain and high winds brought Leopold Mozart and his son to Florence on 30th March 1770, where they lodged at the Aquila inn. In the city were many members of the English aristocracy, some on the Grand Tour, and others who were permanently resident in Florence. A picture by Zoffany, painted about this time and now in the royal collection, shows in great detail numerous well known Englishmen at the Uffizi Gallery, among them the long-serving British minister in Florence, Sir Horace Mann. The Mozarts had stayed with his nephew at his house near Canterbury shortly before leaving England five years previously, and it may have been through him and his uncle that Wolfgang was brought to the attention of another English resident, also shown in the picture, Earl Cowper (1738–89).

George, the third earl, had been resident in Florence for many years and he continued to live there for the rest of his life. During this time his musical connections were such that he acted as agent to the King's Theatre in London for the provision of Italian singers.[1] He was sufficiently wealthy to have his own orchestra, and it was his custom to give lavish musical concerts at his house, the Villa Palmieri, for the benefit of the nobility. One was arranged on the day of the Mozarts' arrival and Wolfgang was invited to perform, together with other eminent musicians, before the earl's friends. Unfortunately, because of the wretched journey from Bologna Wolfgang had contracted a cold, and, always solicitous about his son's health, Leopold confined him to bed. But playing at that concert, which Wolfgang had to forego, was a young English boy, Thomas Linley, who had already acquired a great reputation in Italy as a violinist.

Thomas Linley

Tom Linley was born in Bath in 1756 and was therefore the same age as Mozart. There were many other similarities. Linley's father, Thomas Linley senior, was also a musician, being harpsichordist, composer and director of music in Bath. Tom also had an elder sister, Elizabeth, who was the most outstanding soloist soprano of her time. Like Leopold Mozart, Linley senior was very ambitious for his children's career; Tom had appeared in public when he was seven years old at a concert in Bath where he sang and played the violin.[2] His first London performance was at Covent Garden in January 1767 when, in the presence of the child Prince of Wales, he appeared with his sister Elizabeth in the masque *The Fairy Favour* by J. C. Bach.[3] They were the eldest of a family of eight children, all but one of whom were trained in music, including two other sisters who were also renowned sopranos. Gainsborough was a close friend of the family in Bath and painted portraits of the Linley children, including Thomas, several times. Their handsome appearance, magnificently displayed by Gainsborough in these portraits, their prominence in the world of music, the elopement of Elizabeth with the famous playwright Richard Brinsley Sheridan and her subsequent marriage to him, made the Linley family famous; the fact that five of them died tragically young only enhanced their romantic appeal thereafter.[4]

Young Thomas studied composition with the Master of the King's Music, William Boyce, for five years. In summer 1768 his father sent him to Leghorn to continue his studies with the eminent Italian violinist and composer Pietro Nardini (1722–93), who, in 1770, became director of music at the ducal court in Florence, taking Tom Linley with him. Nardini regarded him as his favourite pupil and under his influence Linley's playing of the violin took on the fine tone and the expressiveness characterised by his master. Il Tommasino, as he was known, became recognised throughout Italy as a true virtuoso on the violin, and he was much in demand for performances at private houses of the nobility, often playing with Nardini. It was on one of these occasions that he was invited to take part in Earl Cowper's concert at the end of March 1770.

Only four days later Tom was called again to perform at a concert in Florence. On this occasion it was given by a certain Signora Maddalena Morelli-Fernandez, who styled herself Corilla Olympica.[5] This flamboyant lady was well known to the Florentine intelligentsia as an 'improvisatrice', which meant that she improvised verses and accompanied them herself on the violin. According to Charles Burney, who was a frequent visitor to her salon, she was an accomplished violinist, on some occasions performing with Nardini and Burney himself.[6] She frequently held conversaziones for the intellectuals of Florence at her house in the Via Cerretani, near San Lorenzo, which were much attended by foreigners, including Il Tommasino. It was here, at the house of la Corilla, that the young Linley met the young Mozart.

In a letter to his wife in Salzburg, Leopold Mozart says that the two boys were attracted to each other immediately, and that on the occasion of this first encounter they performed alternately throughout the evening before the distinguished assembly. He says "this boy, who plays most beautifully, is the same age and the same size as Wolfgang". The following day, Tom Linley, "a most charming boy", visited the Mozarts in their rooms at the Aquila Inn, bringing his violin, and the boys played violin duets the whole afternoon. Leopold goes on to say "on the next day we lunched with M. Gavard, the administrator of the grand ducal finances, and these two boys played in turn the whole afternoon, not like boys, but like men!"[7] What they played is not recorded, but by this time in his career Tom Linley had already composed a number of works for the violin, including at least seven sonatas, some of which he presumably introduced to his friend Mozart. After the end of the recital Tom accompanied father and son home, but he was then much distressed to learn that they were leaving Florence the following day.

At nine o'clock on the morning of their departure, 6th April, Tom came to see Wolfgang and presented him with a farewell poem which he had commissioned la Corilla to write for him the previous evening. The result is scarcely an example of great poetry, but it expresses his joy at their meeting, his wonder at Wolfgang's music and his fond hope that they will see each other again.[8]

E'er since I by fate was divided from thee,
In thought I have followed thy journey in vain;
To tears then laughter and joy turned for me,
Scarce allayed by the hope I may see thee again.

What ecstasies open to music my heart,
By harmony wafted to Eden, forsooth!
To Heaven transported by love of thy art,
I seem for the first time to contemplate truth.

O fortunate instant! O thrice blessed day,
When first I beheld thee, and wondering heard,
By thy music enchanted more than I can say,
Was happy to find myself loved and preferred.
May the gods grant that I shall remember alway
To resemble thy virtues in deed and in word.

In token of sincere esteem and affection
Thomas Linley.

The young Linley then embraced his friend and, with tearful emotion, accompanied the Mozarts' carriage as far as the city gate.

The Mozarts planned to return to Florence, on their way back from their visits to Rome and Naples but in a letter Wolfgang wrote to Tom Linley in September of that year he says that, unfortunately, his father had suffered a serious injury to his leg in an accident to their carriage and was laid up for a long time in Bologna, preventing them from coming to Florence again. He goes on to say that he would do everything in his power to have the pleasure of embracing his dear friend. He ends the letter, "Keep me in your friendship and believe that my affection for you will endure for ever and that I am your most devoted servant and loving friend".[9] This letter was treasured by Linley until his death.

In fact, Mozart never did see his friend again. In the same September,

Charles Burney visited Florence and met Tom Linley several times. In the account of his travels in Italy, Burney describes the elegant, aristocratic life the young Englishman was leading in Florence, but at the same time he says, "After dinner little Linley came to see me, he has been two years under Nardini and is universally admired. The Tommasino, as he is called, and the little Mozart are talked of all over Italy as the most promising geniuses of this age".[10]

In spite of the short duration of their time together, there is little doubt of Mozart's warm affection for the young Englishman. Until now he had been starved of friendship with boys of his own age. All his life his contacts outside the family had been with adults for the purpose of furthering his musical education. It is therefore not surprising that when he met Tom he was attracted by the Linley charm, and in this fourteen-year-old boy, like himself a musician of precocious talent, he found a kindred spirit.

The young Linley remained with Nardini in Florence for a further year and returned to England in autumn 1771 to take part in his father's concerts in Bath, where he was first violinist. During the following Lent he performed in the oratorio season, playing his own violin sonatas and concertos between the acts of the oratorios, as was the custom. By 1773 he was performing in a similar manner at Drury Lane. It is clear from contemporary newspaper accounts that he was now regarded as one of the finest violinists in the country but, increasingly, he turned his attention to composition. During the next three years he produced at least twenty violin concertos as well as many vocal works.[11] During 1773 he wrote 'In Yonder Grove,' a cantata in six movements, sung at the Little Theatre, Haymarket, on 12th March by his sister Elizabeth who also wrote the words. The following morning she married Richard Brinsley Sheridan, never to perform in public again. In the same year came Tom's first major choral work, a fine anthem, 'Let God Arise', which was written for the Three Choirs Festival. It displays extraordinarily accomplished contrapuntal writing for a composer barely seventeen years old. In 1775 he made his first attempt at writing opera, with considerable success. His brother-in-law Sheridan had written the libretto for his opera *The Duenna* and at first asked Linley senior to provide the music. This was the last of the really successful pasticcio operas, first performed on 21st November 1775, at Covent Garden, but it has become apparent over the last few years that it was actually Linley junior who was responsible for most of the newly composed music, amounting to nearly half of the total, including the three movement overture, and for carrying out the arrangements, in the galant style, of the old tunes. Full instrumentation for only the last act remains, but a complete vocal score exists so that the excellent libretto and the quality of the music make a modern revival of *The Duenna* a distinct possibility.

By 1776 Sheridan had become manager of the Drury Lane Theatre and Thomas Linley senior left Bath to be its musical director. For the Lent oratorio season there Tom wrote perhaps his best surviving choral work, *A Lyric Ode on the Fairies, Aerial Beings and Witches of Shakespeare*, for sixty performers. The expressive music, evocative of the supernatural in Shakespeare's plays, received great acclaim and a reviewer in the *Morning Chronicle* the next day, 21st March 1776, maintained it "to be an extraordinary effort of genius in so young a man". He continued working with his father, and in January 1777 he wrote some excellent music for chorus and soprano as an accompaniment to Sheridan's version of *The Tempest*. Later in the year came his oratorio, *The Song of Moses* for Drury Lane, much influenced by Handel. His last surviving work, an opera, *The Cady of Baghdad*, written in 1778, suffers from an inferior libretto but it has recently received a revival.

Several music critics have commented upon similarities between the music of Mozart and that of Linley, particularly in *The Duenna* and in the beautiful aria 'Ariel, who sees thee now' from the *Ode*, to name two examples. It is difficult to believe that the short duration of their meeting would have produced a profound mutual effect on their music, although Einstein speculates that Linley may have introduced Mozart to violin works which influenced his future compositions for the instrument.[12] A likely reason for apparent similarities is that each was affected by the style of composers they had both experienced in Italy and in London, notably that of J. C. Bach.

Regrettably, much of the younger Linley's large output was not published during his lifetime and has not survived, but enough remains to show that he was set to become the major English composer of the latter part of the eighteenth century.

In 1778 Tom and his younger sister Mary were invited by the Duke and Duchess of Ancaster to stay at their country estate, Grimsthorpe Castle in Lincolnshire to take part in the musical activities there. The duchess was very fond of music and it was at her London house in Berkeley Square that she had met the Mozarts during their stay in London. Today, the castle, with its frontage by Vanbrugh, is an imposing building and looks out towards a large lake. On 7th August, Tom, with two companions, decided to go sailing, but as they reached the middle of the lake a sudden squall blew up. They capsized and, in an impetuous attempt to swim for the shore, Tom was drowned. He was buried at the Ancaster parish church at Edenbridge in Lincolnshire.

Thus, the most talented member of the brilliant Linley family died at age twenty two, and England was deprived of the finest musical composer it had produced for nearly a century.

Mozart never forgot him. Years later the Irish singer, Michael Kelly, tells us that when he was in Vienna, in 1784, he was in conversation with Mozart who spoke a good deal about Thomas Linley and their meeting in Florence with great affection. He said that Linley was a true genius; and he felt that, had he lived, he would have been one of the greatest ornaments of the musical world.[13]

﴾ CHAPTER VIII ﴿

ROME

William Beckford, Charles Stuart

T NOON ON 11TH APRIL 1770 LEOPOLD AND HIS SON ARRIVED IN ROME
from Florence after a five-day journey through rain and storms.
During the journey they had to stay in the most horrible, filthy
inns where "we got nothing to eat save here and there eggs and broc-
coli". In fact, it had been continually raining in that part of the country
for four months. In the afternoon they both went to the Sistine Chapel
to hear the famous *Miserere* of Gregorio Allegri. This was the notable
occasion when, according to Leopold, Wolfgang wrote out the entire
work from memory after one hearing. Although Leopold claimed that
his son had carried out this remarkable feat because the Pope had forbidden any publication of the *Miserere*, he was stretching the truth here;
copies of the work did exist as Charles Burney testifies.[1]

William Beckford

Rome was often regarded as the highlight of the Grand Tour, so the city
was full of the English. They tended to congregate especially in the
Piazza di Spagna and to frequent the English coffee house there, but not
all were in pursuit of culture. As the eighteenth-century traveller
Charles de Brosses noted disdainfully,

*The money that the English spend at Rome and the practice of making a
journey there, which forms a part of their education do not profit much the
majority of them. There are some of them who are persons of intelligence
and endeavour to instruct themselves, but these form no great number. The
majority have a hired carriage harnessed at the Piazza di Spagna that is at
their service throughout the day until they go together to play billiards, or
some other similar amusement. I see some of them who will leave Rome
without having seen any but English people and without knowing where the
Coliseum is.*[2]

At the top of the Spanish steps which lead up out of the Piazza di

Spagna, in a street to the left, is what, a century later, Henry James called "perhaps the most enchanting place in Rome"—the gardens of the Villa Medici.[3] Considering the predilection of the English for this area of Rome it is not surprising that ten days after the Mozarts' arrival Leopold reports,

We have met a great many Englishmen here and amongst others Mr Beckford, whose acquaintance we made at Lady Effingham's in London, and with whom we walked for a couple of hours this morning in the garden of the Villa Medici, which belongs to the Grand Duke of Florence.[4]

By this time the Medici family was no more and the Grand Duke was now an Austrian, later to become Emperor Leopold II.

The name Beckford was very well known in eighteenth-century London. The first William (1710–70) was the famous Lord Mayor of London whose sister, Elizabeth, had married Earl Effingham. On the death of Alderman Beckford in 1770 at Fonthill, in Wiltshire, his only legitimate son, also William (1760–1844), inherited his great estates in Jamaica and in England, which at the age of nine made him one of the wealthiest persons in England.[5] Confusingly, however, the friend of the Mozarts was yet another William Beckford, who was the illegitimate son of Alderman Beckford's younger brother Richard, and he was therefore a cousin of the young heir of Fonthill. He also inherited from his father plantations in Jamaica, where he lived for some thirteen years before returning to England to take up residence in Somerley, near Lowestoft, Suffolk. Mozart's Beckford can therefore be distinguished as William Beckford of Somerley.

Lady Elizabeth Effingham (1725–91), the aunt of both younger Beckfords, was Lady of the Bedchamber to Queen Charlotte. She is mentioned in Leopold Mozart's London notebook, and it was at her house in St James's Place, London, that Leopold says he first met William Beckford of Somerley, probably at a concert she had arranged.

At the time when Mozart met Beckford in Italy, he was doing the Grand Tour. Like many other young Englishmen intent on collecting Italian art, he visited the well-known resident English art dealer, Gavin Hamilton, who sold him several choice Old Masters. Five months later Charles Burney on his quest for information for his projected history of music also encountered Beckford in Rome. Burney became very friendly with Beckford, who accompanied him everywhere, introducing him to many English friends long resident in the city, and through them he gained entrance to sources of material useful for his enterprise. When Burney returned to England and, subsequently, in 1776, published the first volume of his epic work by subscription, Beckford was sufficiently enthusiastic to take five copies. It is partly through Burney that this more shadowy William Beckford becomes better known.

Beckford's thirteen-year residence in Jamaica resulted in the publication of two books devoted to the country, *Remarks on the Situation of the Negroes in Jamaica* (1788) and *A Definitive Account of the Island of Jamaica* (1790), for which he is still remembered. However, like that of his much wealthier younger cousin, the Fonthill William, the income from the Jamaican estates declined severely, and he had to leave his home at Somerley Hall. On 23rd January 1789 there was an auction at Christie's in London of William of Somerley's pictures to meet his debts. The sale of his "capital and well known collection of Italian, French, Flemish, and Dutch pictures collected at liberal expense during his travels abroad" fetched £1255.[6] His cousin had helped him on more than one occasion to escape from the clutches of the creditors, but in 1791 he was committed to the Fleet prison for debt.

Charles Burney remembered him with affection. Fanny Burney says in her *Memoirs of Doctor Burney*,

The unfortunate, but truly amiable and high-minded Mr Beckford was among the greatest favourites and most welcome visitors to Dr. Burney; whose remembrance of the friendly zeal of that gentleman in Italy was a never failing call for every soothing return that could be offered to him in the calamities which, roughly and ruinously, had now changed his whole situation in life—leaving his virtues alone unalterable.[7]

Burney himself visited Beckford in the Fleet, and in a letter to Fanny in October 1791 he described his visit:

I intend to try to get Sir Joshua (Reynolds) and Sir Joseph Banks, his old acquaintances, to visit him there with me. I was with the dear, worthy, and charming man, two hours on Wednesday, and love him and honour him more than ever. What a place—surrounded with fresh horrors!—for the habitation of such a man.[8]

Subsequently Beckford and his wife Charlotte took up residence in Sloane Street, Chelsea,[9] and he was a frequent visitor at the house of another cousin, the current Earl Effingham, in Wimpole Street, London. It was here on 5th February 1799 that William Beckford, historian of Jamaica, and friend of Mozart, died.[10]

While there is no doubt of Mozart's connection with William Beckford of Somerley, there is a curious story of a possible link between Mozart and the far more famous William Beckford of Fonthill, not in Italy, but in England. This William, known as 'England's wealthiest son', at age twenty was the author of the fantastic, oriental novel *Vathek*, for which he is best known. An eccentric, a dilettante, an art collector and a member of Parliament, he used his great inherited wealth to re-build the family mansion, Fonthill, on an incredibly lavish scale complete with a three-hundred-foot Gothic tower. He renamed the mansion Fonthill Abbey. But the enormous cost of the building, together with the decline in Jamaica's economy which had been so disastrous for his cousin, were too much even for the author of *Vathek*. In 1822 Fonthill had to be sold. Beckford retired to a smaller but still spacious house in Bath where, surrounded by his books and art collection, he died in April 1844 at the age of eighty-four.

Among Beckford's many interests was music; all his life he was a great admirer of Mozart's works. After his death, his numerous personal papers were found to contain a letter written about 1840 in which, referring to Mozart, Beckford says,

He passed some time at Fonthill, having been engaged, though quite a child, to give me—his junior by four or five years—lessons of composition. We re-newed our acquaintance at Vienna, where I found him as strange, as melan-choly, but more wonderful than ever.[11]

However, he heightens the absurdity in a further statement when he maintains that during those lessons he was responsible for Mozart composing the famous aria 'Non piu andrai' from *Le nozze di Figaro*. The extraordinary assertion of this William Beckford that he, at the age of four or five, had lessons from Mozart when he was in England at the age of eight to nine, has no confirmation in any of the Mozart family correspondence. Indeed, the tenor of Beckford's description of Mozart as "strange and melancholy" at the age of eight or nine just does not ring true. Beckford himself could certainly be described as strange, as well as being charged with an imagination capable of producing *Vathek*. It is quite possible that he did actually encounter Mozart, together with his cousin, at the house of their aunt Lady Effingham in London, but it would seem that long afterwards he embellished their meeting to portray a familiarity with the now famous composer. As C. B. Oldman pointed out, in his analysis of the curious affair, it is very unlikely that Leopold Mozart would have omitted mentioning the name of William Beckford of Fonthill if he, the son of the wealthy and powerful Lord Mayor of London, had been instructed by Wolfgang.

Charles Stuart, The Young Pretender

On the tenth day of their stay in Rome the Mozarts were invited to the house of Prince Chigi, where it still stands in the Piazza Colonna. It was here in the Golden Hall of this imposing palace that Wolfgang played at a concert arranged by the prince. Of this performance, Baron Saint-Odile, the Tuscan ambassador, writes, "Last night, I heard Young Mozart at the House of Prince Chigi; he is truly a prodigy of nature, all those present at the Conversazione immensely admiring his excellence in music".[12] Amongst those listening was, according to Leopold, "the so-called King of England or Pretender". A week later the Mozarts again met "The King of England" at the great baroque Palazzo Barberini, home of the Princess Barberini-Colonna.

After the death of his father, the Old Pretender, in 1766, Charles Edward Stuart (1720–1788), self-styled King Charles III, had returned to live in Rome at the Palazzo Muti where he had been born forty six years earlier. When the Mozarts met him in 1770, twenty-five years had passed since he had first raised the Jacobite standard as Bonnie Prince Charlie, and ever since his escape from Scotland a year later he had drifted between France and Italy, endlessly seeking recognition of his royal status. Brought up in Rome, he was, from an early age, interested in music, and he was an accomplished cellist. The French traveller Charles de Brosses heard him as a youth play one of his favourite pieces, Corelli's Concerto Grosso No. 8 in G minor, with his brother on the violin. He was a frequent visitor to the opera and the many private concerts which were given in the houses of the Roman nobility, where he was often to be found asleep. By this time the Young Pretender, at age fifty, was suffering from serious ill health. Prone to fits of depression and uncontrollable rages, he was now showing the signs of chronic alcoholism. Lady Anne Miller, a contemporary English traveller, describes his appearance at the time the Mozarts would have encountered him—dressed in a scarlet coat, trimmed with gold lace and wearing the blue Order of the Garter:

He is naturally above the middle size but stoops excessively; he appears bloated and red in the face, his countenance heavy and sleepy, which is attributed to his having given into excess of drinking; but when a young man he must have been esteemed handsome. His complexion is of the fair tint, his eyes blue, his hair light brown, and the contour of his face a long oval; he is by no means thin, has a noble presence, and a graceful manner.[13]

But, in spite of this physical decline, it would be another eighteen years before the unhappy Charles Edward Stuart died at the Palazzo Muti.

FIG. 6. William Hamilton (1730–1803) and his wife Catherine. Painting by David Allan, 1770. *From the Blair Castle Collection, Perthshire.*

NAPLES

William Vyse, Sir William Hamilton, Catherine Hamilton

E ARLY IN THEIR ITALIAN TOUR, LEOPOLD HAD SIGNALLED THEIR INTEN-
tion of their going to Naples, "which is such an important centre".
Naples had become the leading city of opera in Italy during the first
part of the eighteenth century due to Alessandro Scarlatti (1660–1725),
who was prominent in the development of opera seria, and the young Giovanni Pergolesi (1710–36), who was an early exponent of opera buffa, together with their successors such as Niccolò Piccinni (1728–1800) and
Nicolò Jommelli (1714–74). The fact that Wolfgang had now been commissioned to compose an opera, *Mitridate, rè di Ponto*, for Milan at
Christmas, made it more imperative than ever that they should visit Naples.

Leaving Rome on the morning of 8th May, father and son travelled south
in a two-seater carriage by the road through the Pontine marshes on a
leisurely six day journey. They avoided the horrors of the roadside inns in
this part of Italy by staying at Augustinian monasteries.

After their arrival in Naples on 14th May they lost no opportunity in attending the magnificent opera house of San Carlo. Burney describes its
"noble and elegant structure":

*There are 7 rows of boxes sufficient to hold 10 or 12 persons in each. . . . In the
front of each box there is a mirror 3 or 4 feet long by 2 or 3 wide, before which
are two large wax tapers. These by reflexion being multiplied and added to the
lights of the stage and to those within the boxes make it too much for the aching
sight.*[1]

In these impressive surroundings father and son heard the celebrated
Neopolitan singers Anna Lucia de Amicis and Giuseppe Aprile singing
Jommelli's latest opera, *Armida abbandonata*. But the fourteen-year-old
Wolfgang already showed his critical ability when he wrote to his sister,
"The opera here is one of Jommelli's; it is beautiful, but too serious and old
fashioned for the theatre. De Amicis sings amazingly well and so does
Aprile, who sang in Milan. The dances are wretchedly pompous. The the-
atre is beautiful".[2] Three years later Wolfgang was able to persuade Signora

de Amicis to take the role of prima donna in his own laſt theatrical work for Milan, *Lucio Silla*.

Then, as now, Naples was a city of contraſts which Leopold Mozart emphasises when writing to his wife,

The situation of the town, the fruitfulness of the country, the liveliness of the people, the rare sights and a hundred beautiful things make me sorry to leave. But the filth, the crowds of beggars, the hateful and godless populace, the disgraceful way in which children are brought up, the incredible frivolity even in the churches, make it possible quite calmly to leave behind what is good.[3]

It was the "good" of Naples, with a population of three hundred thousand, the largeſt city in Italy, which attraċted the English on the Grand Tour. It had much to offer, because in addition to the exciting life of the city there were the speċtacular geographical sights of Vesuvius and the bay, and, for some, the round of parties in the palazzos of expatriate Englishmen. Seekers of culture could enjoy the recently discovered marvels of Herculaneum and Pompeii, an enthusiasm shared by the Mozarts: "On Monday and Tuesday we are going to Vesuvius, Pompeii, Herculaneum and its excavations, Caserta and Capo di Monte. All this is going to coſt money."[4]

William Vyse

A week after their arrival, Leopold writes that they again met William Beckford, this time in the company of another of their London acquaintances, whom he calls "Mr Weis". When he was in Rome, Burney refers to a companion of Beckford by the name of a Mr Vyse, "an agreeable young gent.", who had been colleċting Neopolitan music material for him. He adds that the young man was about to return to England on account of the recent death of his father. This points to the identity of Leopold Mozart's Mr Weis as William Vyse (1742–1816), whose family came from Lichfield. After his education at Brasenose College, Oxford, the young Vyse went to London where he met the Mozart family and also became friendly with a Dr John Bevis, lawyer and antiquary, who was inſtrumental in his introduċtion to Charles Burney in Rome. There, he and Beckford spent much time dining in the company of Burney and the English expatriates before his Grand Tour was cut short by his father's death. After his return to England Vyse entered the Church, becoming, two years later, canon of Lichfield. He subsequently rose to importance by being elected a Fellow of the Royal Society in 1781, then archdeacon of Coventry and, finally, chancellor of Lichfield.[5]

Sir William Hamilton

The meeting with Beckford and Vyse took place on 18th May, when the Mozarts called at the Palazzo Sessa, the town house of the most distinguished Englishman in Naples, the British Ambassador, the Honourable (later Sir) William Hamilton and his wife Catherine.[6] Their house, with its magnificent view towards the bay, was always full of visitors, especially the English, and here the Hamiltons were able to indulge their musical interests. They had their own private box at the San Carlo theatre and William Hamilton, himself, had studied the violin with Giardini in London. But it was his wife who was the leading musical influence. Lady Anne Miller, on visiting the Palazzo Sessa in January 1771, remarked that she could have found herself at an assembly in London:

Mrs Hamilton's musical assembly which she gives once a week is rendered perfect by her elegant taste and fine performance; it is called an Accademia di Musica; and I suppose no country can produce a more complete band of excellent performers.[7]

When the Mozarts set foot in the Hamilton household they must have cut striking figures in their new summer outfits. The stern-faced father was dressed in a cinnamon-coloured suit made of piqued Florentine cloth with silver lace and lined with apple-green silk. Accompanying him was his lively young son in a suit of flame coloured moiré, also trimmed with silver lace but lined with sky-blue silk.

One of the ambassador's close expatriate friends who shared his interests in art and music was the young nobleman, Kenneth Mackenzie, Viscount Fortrose (1744–81), whose house in Naples included a splendid music room. It appears that William Hamilton introduced the Mozarts to him because there is a picture of the music room painted in 1771 by Pietro Fabris, now in the Scottish National Portrait Gallery, in which there is a quartet which has been identified as Mozart playing a small spinet, his father playing the harpsichord, William Hamilton playing the violin, and the violinist Gaetano Pugnani. Lord Fortrose stands looking on approvingly.[8]

William Hamilton (1730–1803) became British ambassador to the court of Naples in November 1764 and had met the Mozarts in London shortly before taking up his appointment. In addition to being an experienced diplomat he had become a world authority on volcanoes, and his lean, athletic figure was to be seen climbing Vesuvius on many occasions. He carried out detailed studies on the phenomena of the eruptions and published his observations in several volumes as well as communications to the Royal Society, of which he was made a Fellow. A man of many interests, William Hamilton was also renowned as an antiquary and was closely concerned with the excavations at the recently discovered Herculaneum and Pompeii. He amassed a vast collection of ancient Greek and Roman vases, terracottas, glass, bronzes and coins, which were displayed in a series of rooms at the Palazzo Sessa but, on a return visit to London in 1772, he sold them to the British Museum for the sum of £8,400, thereby providing the basis of the Museum's great Greek and Roman collection. At one time he owned the famous Portland vase, which, later, was also acquired by the British Museum. In 1772, while he was in London, he was created Knight of the Bath. After his wife Catherine's death in 1782, he paid another visit to England. It was on this occasion that he was introduced to a Miss Emma Hart, the mistress of his favourite nephew, the Hon. Charles Greville. In 1791 Sir William married Emma Hart, who was the complete antithesis of Catherine, and she became the notorious second Lady Hamilton, of Nelson fame.

Sir William Hamilton ended his assignment as British plenipotentiary to Naples in 1800, having served there for thirty-six years. He died at his London home in Piccadilly three years later in the presence of his wife Emma with, reputedly, Nelson holding his hand.

Catherine Hamilton

The Mozarts were particularly attracted by Hamilton's first wife, Catherine. Reporting their visit to William Hamilton on the evening of 18th May, Leopold says that his wife

plays the clavier with unusual feeling and is a very pleasant person. She trembled at having to play before Wolfgang. She has a valuable instrument, made in England by Tschudi, which has two manuals and a pedal, so that the two manuals can be disconnected by the action of the foot.[9]

On his visit to Naples, Charles Burney also attests to the ability of Catherine Hamilton when he says, "Mrs H. has a very neat finger and plays the harpsichord with great delicacy, expression and taste".[10] Ten days after her meeting with Wolfgang, Catherine Hamilton arranged for him to give a concert at the house of the Viennese imperial ambassador, Count Kaunitz. The concert was a great success, and Leopold says it brought in a useful sum, about one hundred and fifty zecchini.[11] The tickets were priced at two and a half zecchini each, (about £40) which indicates an audience of sixty wealthy Neapolitans.

Catherine, the daughter of Hugh Barlow, a wealthy Pembrokeshire squire, had married the Hon. William Hamilton in 1758. In many respects it was a happy marriage, but her life was plagued by illness. It seems that it was his wife's health that influenced Hamilton to move from London to the warmth of Naples. She was a shy, reserved person and her music compensated for the many absences of her husband on official state business at the Neopolitan court or when he was accompanying the king on his frequent hunting trips. She was nonetheless regarded by Burney as being "very sensible". Her quiet sense is shown later in the long conversations she had with the young, emotionally disturbed William Beckford of Fonthill, when, on his Grand Tour, he also visited Sir William and his wife in 1780. Beckford describes Catherine Hamilton's playing: "No performer that I ever heard produced such soothing effects. They seemed the emanations of a pure, uncontaminated mind, at peace with itself and benevolently desirous of diffusing that happy tranquillity around it".[12] She continued to correspond with him giving him sound advice about the wayward nature of his life for the next two years. In 1782 William Beckford of Fonthill returned to Naples only to find Catherine Hamilton desperately ill. To his great distress, on 25th August she died of a fever in the presence of her grieving husband at their country house, the Villa Angelica, at Portici.

FIG. 7. Charles Burney (1726–1814). Portrait by Sir Joshua Reynolds, 1781.
By courtesy of the National Portrait Gallery, London.

BOLOGNA
Charles Burney

LEOPOLD MOZART AND HIS SON VISITED BOLOGNA TWICE. ON THE FIRST occasion, the main object was to make contact with one of the greatest musical figures in all Italy—teacher, composer, and music historian—the Franciscan father Giovanni Battista Martini (1706–84). They arrived on 24th March 1770 from Milan and visited Padre Martini twice during the four days they were in Bologna. On each occasion the great man, an unrivalled authority on counterpoint, tested Wolfgang's ability by getting him to work out several difficult fugues. The result was much to the satisfaction of the master, and, as Leopold proudly states, Wolfgang was admired here more than he had been in all the other towns of Italy.[1]

After this short stay father and son moved on to Florence, Rome and Naples, and it was on the return journey that Leopold suffered a severe injury to his right leg in an accident to their carriage. This event imposed a second, and this time prolonged, stay in Bologna during the summer of 1770. It was then that they encountered Charles Burney.

Born Charles Macburney at Shrewsbury on 7th April 1726, Charles Burney, as he was always called, received his early musical education from Edmund Baker, the organist at Chester Cathedral who introduced him to Thomas Arne. Then aged eighteen, he was apprenticed to Arne as an unpaid musical assistant, transcribing his master's compositions and playing in the orchestra when required. Much of the work was sheer drudgery but, by reason of the fact that his master was the leading English composer of the time, he came to the notice of the aristocratic figure Fulke Greville, who was sufficiently impressed to buy him out of his apprentice-ship. Thereafter Burney's life changed completely. His wealthy patron introduced him to the great and the good in the world of music, literature and the arts, and with his own natural ability and his social graces he moved easily into London society. He soon obtained appointments as organist and composer for Drury Lane and he became a fashionable music teacher. However, in 1751 he received a setback when serious ill health forced him to leave London and to take the position of organist in remote King's Lynn.

But even here Burney was received with cordialty by the local aristocracy and, now married, he and his wife led a very full social life.

In 1760, his health having improved, he returned to resume his career in London. His lively mind and convivial manner continued to bring him into contact with the famous, so that he was able to include as his close friends men such as Garrick, Johnson, Boswell and Reynolds. Never a composer of any distinction, his interest was, by now, in music criticism and music history. Early in 1770 Burney was installed as Doctor of Music at Oxford University, and he states that it was at this time that he was seized with the idea of writing a comprehensive history of music. He wrote to a friend in May 1770:

It is somewhat extraordinary that nothing of the kind has been attempted in our language. . . . I have therefore determined to fly to Italy this summer and to allay my thirst of knowledge at the pure source. . . . No one that I know of has gone into Italy merely upon such an errand, though the Italians at present surpass the rest of Europe in no one art so much as in their music.[2]

On 5th June 1770 Charles Burney sailed from Dover to Calais and thence to Paris, from where he travelled south through France to Geneva and then crossed over the Mont Cenis to enter his beloved Italy. Armed with introductions from his influential friends in England, he journeyed to Turin, Milan, Vicenza, Padua and Venice, gathering information all the way on many aspects of Italian music. In Venice he was able to buy, to his great delight, the first volume of a 'History of Music' published thirteen years before by Padre Martini. While he was greatly enamoured of Venice and its rich store of music, his determined object was to reach Bologna to meet the great Padre Martini in person and to tap his wealth of musical knowledge.

He arrived in Bologna on 21st August. His first impression was that the city looked melancholy, but he added that parts of it were very magnificent and beautiful. Looking around him at the abundant fruit for sale so cheaply in the streets he commented, "The trade here is chiefly that of the belly. The people are very poor but fat and contented".[3]

Padre Martini was now sixty-four and not in very good health, but he welcomed Burney with invitations to visit him as often as he wished. As expected, he was immensely helpful to the enterprise in supplying information on historical as well as contemporary music and providing further useful contacts in Italy. His kindness impressed Burney, "Upon so short an acquaintance I never liked a man more."[4]

Having achieved his ambition, Burney was preparing to leave for Florence when Padre Martini suggested that he stay a little longer to attend a very important annual event which was sure to interest him. This was the Mass and Vespers in the Church of San Giovanni in Monte given by the members of the celebrated Bologna Accademia Filharmonica.

By 20th July Leopold Mozart and his son had arrived back in Bologna, where the elder Mozart decided to rest his injured leg. It was particularly welcome, therefore, when, two weeks later, they were invited by the Count Gian Luca Pallavicini to stay with his family in their luxurious country house just outside the city. In these delightful surroundings Leopold steadily recovered and Wolfgang became very friendly with the young Pallavicini heir, a boy of his own age.

On 1st September Leopold writes to his wife:

His Excellency (Count Pallavacini) arranged for us to be driven into town on the 30th in order to hear the Mass and Vespers of the Accademia Filharmonica, which had been composed by ten different members; that is to say, one wrote the Kyrie and Gloria, another the Credo, and so forth. Thus each psalm of the vespers was set to music by a different Kapellmeister, who in each case conducted his own composition. But they all had to be members of the Academy.[5]

Charles Burney now takes up the story:

I went to S. Giovanni in Monte to hear the Philharmonic performances. There was a great deal of company and who should I meet but the celebrated little German, Mozart, who in 1766 [actually 1764] astonished all the hearers in London by his premature musical talent. I had a long conversation with his father. I find they are inmates at the Palace of Prince Palaviccini. The little man is grown considerably but is still a little man. He has been at Rome and Naples, where he was much admired. At Rome the Pope has conferred on him the Order of the Speron d'Oro, or Gold Spur, the only civil or military order in the gift of his Holiness. He astonished the Italian musicians wherever he stopt. He is now at the age of 12 [actually 14], ingaged to compose an Opera for Milan, on occasion of the marriage of the Principessina of Modena with one of the Arch-Dukes of Austria. There are to be 3 new operas composed on this occasion. I know not yet who are his concurrents; but shall be curious to know how this extraordinary boy acquits himself in setting words in a language not his own. But there is no musical excellence which I do not expect from his extraordinary quickness and talents, under the guidance of so able a musician and intelligent a man as his father, who, I was informed, had been ill five or six weeks at Bologna.[6]

Thereupon they parted. Burney made his farewells to Padre Martini and proceeded to Florence where he was to meet and become very well acquainted with Mozart's English friend Linley, with whom he talked a great deal, extolling both him and the young Mozart as true geniuses.

The Mozarts remained in Bologna for a further six weeks when Wolfgang, after being subjected to a testing examination, was himself installed, at the unheard of age of fourteen, as a member of the exclusive Accademia Filharmonica.

Charles Burney, following the example of the Mozarts, left Florence for Rome, and finally to Naples where he was entertained by the English ambassador William Hamilton and his wife Catherine, who had already been excellent hosts to Leopold and his son. After a stay in Naples of three months, meeting the important figures of Italian opera and accumulating material for his book, he set out on the long return journey to England, arriving back in London on 7th November 1770.

Burney's great passion for Italy and the vast amount of information he had garnered on his journey appears in his book *The Present State of Music in France and Italy*, published in the year after he returned from his travels.[7] The book was received with great acclaim by his contemporaries in London, including Dr Johnson who remarked that he was much aware of his friend Dr Burney's book when he wrote his own *Journey to the Western Isles of Scotland*. However, Burney is remembered most for his great *History of Music*, in four volumes. It ranges widely in time and geography, but it gives a disproportionate amount of space to Italian music, especially opera, at the expense of all other countries, including his own native England.[8]

In a notebook, written in 1771, Burney has entries on Mozart which were intended to be included in the fourth volume of the *History* but, for unknown reasons, were not published. These describe what he heard and saw at the Mozart lodgings in London and at the house of the prominent Jewish musical amateur and Fellow of the Royal Society, Naphtali Franks, where Wolfgang had performed. In these notes Burney comments on the child's fondness for Manzuoli, the famous castrato, and his ability to imitate the styles of different opera singers in an extemporary opera to nonsense words, to which he added an overture in three movements, "all full of taste, imagination, with good harmony, melody, and modulation". Tellingly, Burney emphasises the great contrast between these extraordinary achievements and the age of this prodigy by ending "after which he played at marbles in the true childish way of one who knows nothing!"[9]

It is at first sight strange that Burney gives only a passing reference to Mozart in the *History*: "having astounded all of Europe as a prodigy, he is now no less the wonder of the musical world for his fertility and knowledge as a composer".[10] But in his initial lack of appreciation of the mature Mozart, Burney was in company with many of his contemporaries, with the notable exception of Haydn, and it may have been Haydn's unbounded enthusiasm for Mozart that helped to change his views towards the end of his life.

The *History of Music* appeared between 1776 and 1789, but Burney's music writing was not ended. Towards the end of his long life he was asked at age seventy-five by Abraham Rees, a literary editor, to undertake the music component of a new, very large, general encyclopaedia.[11] In his several contributions for the *Cyclopaedia*, which appeared between 1802 and 1819, Burney reveals that his knowledge of Mozart's works came to him late. In his article on 'Symphony' written in 1804, he rhapsodises over the works of Haydn but goes on to say, "All these excellencies the admirable Mozart had nearly attained; and perhaps he is only inferior to Haydn in the number of his symphonies from the shortness of his vital course!"

As far as Mozart's vocal music is concerned, Burney must have heard some of the famous arias which Mozart's friends Thomas Attwood and Stephen Storace had incorporated into their works after their return to London in 1787. These are probably in the mind of Burney when, after the composer's death, he enthusiastically praised the vocal works of Mozart to the Princess of Wales, as described in the chapter on Thomas Attwood. The first performance in London of a whole Mozart opera did not take place until March 1806, when *La clemenza di Tito* was performed at the King's Theatre. This is the only known attendance of Burney at a Mozart opera. There is an entry in his diary for Thursday, 27th March 1806: "Mrs Billington's benefit, the charming Opera 'La clemenza di Tito' by Mozart in which Mrs Billington looked, acted and sang better than I ever heard her, more pathetic than bravura."[12]

In the article on Mozart he wrote for the *Cyclopaedia* in 1813, but published posthumously, Burney retails the story of Haydn's feelings for Mozart:

When Haydn was asked in our hearing by Broderip [the publisher] in his music shop whether Mozart had left any MS compositions behind him that were worth publishing, as his widow had offered his unedited papers at a high price to the principle publishers of music throughout Europe, Haydn eagerly said 'Purchase them by all means. He was a truly great musician. I have been often flattered by my friends with having some genius; but he was much superior'.[13]

A further passage from the *Cyclopaedia* crystallises Burney's thoughts:

In England we knew nothing of his studies or productions, but from his harpsichord lessons, which frequently came over from Vienna; and in these he seems to have been trying experiments. They were full of new passages, and new effects; but were wild, capricious, and not always pleasing. We were wholly unacquainted with his vocal music till after his decease, though it is manifest that by composing for the voice he first refined his taste, and gave way to his feelings, as in his later compositions for the piano forte and other instruments his melody is exquisite, and cherished and enforced by the most judicious accompaniments, equally free from pedantry and caprice.

In 1787 he took up residence at Chelsea Hospital as organist and it was here that he died on 12th April 1814. By modern standards Charles Burney as a balanced critic has severe limitations but as a music historian he provides an essential source of information about music in the eighteenth century.[14]

PART THREE
The English in Vienna

FIG. 8. Michael Kelly (1762–1826) as a young man. Engraving from a watercolour by Thomas Lawrence. *V&A Picture Library.*

❧ CHAPTER XI ❧
MICHAEL KELLY

T HE YEARS 1784 TO 1787 WERE SOME OF THE HAPPIEST AND MOST
productive in Mozart's career. It was during this period in Vienna that
he developed a close attachment to a circle of four musicians, three
from London and one from Dublin, who were to have an important influence on his life. It is due to one of these British friends, the tenor Michael
Kelly, that we have first-hand knowledge of their relationship with Mozart.
Kelly's *Reminiscences* were dictated by him to an amenuensis, Theodore
Hook, and published in 1826. Not always accurate, engagingly self-impor-
tant and maddeningly deficient in chronological detail, these *Reminiscences*,
nevertheless, provide a vivid account of Mozart in the 1780s, life in Vienna
at the time, and the fate of his British friends after their return to the
London musical scene of the late eighteenth century.

Born in Dublin on 25th December 1762, Michael Kelly was the son of
Thomas Kelly, a wine merchant and music lover who was also Master of
Ceremonies at Dublin Castle. Through his father's position he came into
contact early in his life with the many musical figures who visited Dublin,
then a centre of music in Britain second only to London. He started
learning music at age seven and had a series of teachers, mostly Italian.
Among them was the famous castrato Rauzzini, who was so impressed with
the young Kelly's voice that he advised Michael's father to forget all his
ambitions for him to become a surgeon and to send him to Italy to complete his training as a singer. By the time he was fifteen Michael had appeared on the Dublin stage in two operas, one of which was Dibdin's *Lionel
and Clarissa*, in which he took the male name part. By these performances
the young singer earned enough money to finance his visit to Italy. On 1st
May 1779 Michael sailed for Naples, taking with him his own piano; he was
armed with an introduction to the British ambassador to the Neopolitan
court, Sir William Hamilton. He arrived four weeks later and presented his
credentials to Sir William, who, with his wife, the first Lady Hamilton, gave
him a warm welcome. Nine years previously they had similarly entertained
the fourteen-year-old Mozart and his father.

Sir William Hamilton agreed that Kelly should study with the composer of church music and operas, Fedele Fenaroli (1730–1818), at the conservatorio of La Madonna di Loreto in Naples. This decision was largely to satisfy his father's wish that he should study composition and the theory of music in order to return to England as a composer and teacher, whereas his own inclinations were as a singer. However, the young Michael got on well with Fenaroli and it was through him that he was able to attend all the famous opera houses and to gain an entrée to the nobility of Naples. Sir William Hamilton introduced him to the king and queen for whom he was asked to sing at one of their open-air concerts. King Ferdinand IV, not noted for his intellect, was so unaware of the existence of Ireland that he even asked Kelly whether he was a Christian![1]

Time passed very pleasantly and he was an enthusiastic witness of the colourful Neopolitan life. He often passed the mornings singing in the church festivals, where his master was venerated for his church music. Most evenings were spent at the theatre or singing at the private houses of the Italian nobility or of Sir William Hamilton. At one of these houses he met the composer, Cimarosa, who also had been a pupil of Fenaroli. But it was an introduction to the eminent castrato and most famous singing teacher of the time, Giuseppe Aprile (1732–1813) that changed his musical direction. Aprile was so taken with Kelly's vocal ability that he offered to teach him without fee and to take him on a prolonged visit to Sicily, saying, "I have no doubt but that in a short time I can make him capable of earning his bread anywhere".[2]

They left Naples in 1780 and after their arrival in Palermo, Aprile was as good as his word. Kelly says he studied five or six hours every day and in the evening he accompanied his master to the many supper concerts at private houses to which they were invited. He sang in public at the great annual Palermo festival of Santa Rosalia and was a frequent attender at the theatre.

Kelly became very attached to Aprile, but in the following year his master had to return to Naples, leaving his pupil now fully equipped to make his way in the opera houses of Europe. Kelly showed his appreciation by presenting Aprile with his much travelled piano. Many years later, Kelly, never one to miss an occasion for name-dropping, tells of how,

when dining with my dear and lamented friend, the late [second] *Lady Hamilton, at Merton, I had the pleasure of hearing of this circumstance from the illustrious Lord Nelson, near whom I had the honour of being seated at table.*

He said "Kelly, when in Naples, I have frequently heard your old master,
Aprile, speak of you with great affection, though he said, that when you were
with him you were as wild as a colt. He mentioned, also, your having given him
your piano-forte, which, he said, nothing should induce him to part with".[3]

Kelly took ship from Sicily for Leghorn, where he arrived after six days at
sea. It was here as he stepped on to the quay that he encountered the two
people from England, Nancy and Stephen Storace, with whom he was later
to be involved for much of his career.

Finally, he reached Florence and on the strength of letters provided by
Aprile he was engaged to sing at the Teatro Nova, thereby making his
Italian debut in opera. Kelly was also introduced to those long-standing
English expatriates in Florence, Lord and Lady Cowper. Ten years after
the Mozarts had visited the city, the Cowpers were still giving their famed
concerts. It was at their house that Kelly met the great violinist Pietro Nardini, who, although then quite old, recalled to him with great affection his
favourite pupil, the young Thomas Linley, Mozart's friend in 1770.

In June 1782 Kelly's engagement in Florence came to an end and he
made his way to Venice. It was here, in October, that Kelly again met the
young English soprano whom he had last seen in Leghorn, Nancy Storace.
She was now famous, so much so that early in the following year she received the Imperial summons to Vienna. At this point the chronology of
Kelly's career is somewhat confused, but it seems that he continued to stay
in Venice, singing in oratorio in the season of Lent during 1784.

By now Kelly had fully established himself as a top singer in opera buffa
and in the early part of that year he also was informed by the Austrian ambassador that the emperor would like to have his services for the newly
formed Italian theatre company of Vienna. He accepted the invitation with
alacrity at the salary of four hundred ducats, free lodging and fuel, including four large wax candles per day. On his arrival in Vienna Kelly immediately made his acquaintance with the conductor of the Italian opera
and court composer, Antonio Salieri (1750–1825). He describes Mozart's
rival as a little man with an expressive countenance, looking very like
David Garrick, who accompanied him to the very elegant appartment
which had been assigned to him. Salieri informed Kelly that his operatic
debut would be Salieri's own *La scuola dei gelosi*. Two weeks later he performed this work in the company of the star singers Nancy Storace and
Francesco Benucci to the applause of the Emperor. Kelly came to Vienna

equipped with introductions to several important personages, including the British ambassador, Sir Robert Keith, with the result that he received a warm welcome. The young, talkative Irishman, with his engaging manner, soon entered wholeheartedly into the whirl of Viennese life.

Kelly gives a first-hand account of the Vienna with which Mozart was familiar, and the passion for music which the inhabitants enjoyed.[4] He describes the beauty of the women, the magnificent palace buildings, and the parks, especially the Prater, which he compares, greatly to its favour, with Hyde Park. He recounts how one evening he sat at a café on the banks of the Danube in the company of Salieri, discussing a composition, when they were disturbed by a large wild boar crossing the river and making its way towards them, causing them to take to their heels. He describes the love of the Viennese for dancing, which reached its height at the time of the Carnival when even ladies well advanced in pregnancy would dance knowing that facilities were provided on the spot if they were unfortunate enough to give birth! The favourite dance was the Deutscher, or 'German dance', a forerunner of the waltz. Mozart wrote many examples and was himself a most enthusiastic dancer, as his wife confided to Kelly one evening at supper. Only a year previously Mozart had written to his father, "Last week I gave a ball in my own rooms. . . . We began at six in the evening and kept on until seven. What, only an hour? Of course not. Until seven o'clock next morning".[5]

Kelly gives a detailed portrait of his employer, Emperor Joseph II.[6] Passionately devoted to music, he frequently attended the rehearsals of his Opera Company and was at their performances almost every night:

His mode of living was quite methodical. He got up every morning winter and summer at five o'clock, wrote until nine, then took a cup of chocolate and transacted business with his ministers till one. He was very partial to the jeu de paume [a form of tennis] and a good player. He had a fine racket-court, and, when not in it, he usually walked or rode from one till three: punctually at a quarter after three his dinner was served. At five he usually walked in the corridor near his dining room and whilst there was accessible to the complaints of the meanest of his subjects; he heard them with complaisance and was ever ready to redress their grievances. He generally wore either a green or white uniform faced with red; nor did I ever see him that he was not continually putting chocolate drops, which he took from his waistcoat pocket, into his mouth. When he walked out, he took a number of gold sovereigns with him, and distributed them personally among the indigent. He was enemy to pomp and parade, and avoided them as much as possible; indeed any private gentleman requires so little attendance as he did.

Joseph's austere and simple personal life extended into the far-reaching, diverse reforms which he exacted upon the state during his reign, among them, the relinquishment of the long-established privileges of the nobility. This was the ruler whose favours were so important to Mozart.

Kelly met Mozart for the first time at a concert given at the house of the Czech composer, pianist, and music publisher Leopold Kozeluch (1747–1818). He says,

what was to me one of the greatest gratifications of my musical life, was there introduced to that prodigy of genius—Mozart. He favoured the company by performing fantasias and capriccios on the piano-forte. His feeling, the rapidity of his fingers, the great execution and strength of his left hand, particularly, and the apparent inspiration of his modulations, astounded me. After this splendid performance we sat down to supper, and I had the pleasure to be placed at table between him and his wife, Madame Constance Weber, a German lady of whom he was passionately fond, and by whom he had three children. After supper the young branches of our host had a dance, and Mozart joined them. . . . He was a remarkably small man, very thin and pale, with a profusion of fine fair hair, of which he was rather vain. He gave me a cordial invitation to his house, of which I availed myself, and passed a great deal of my time there. He always received me with kindness and hospitality. He was remarkably fond of punch, of which beverage I have seen him take copious draughts. He was also fond of billiards, and had an excellent billiard table in his house. Many and many a game have I played with him, but always came off second best. He gave Sunday concerts, at which I never was missing. He was kind-hearted, and always ready to oblige; but so very particular, when he played, that if the slightest noise were made, he instantly left off. He one day made me sit down to the piano, and gave credit to my first master, who had taught me to place my hand well on the instrument. He conferred on me what I considered a high compliment. I had composed a little melody to Metastasio's canzonetta, 'Grazie agl'inganni tuoi,' which was a great favourite wherever I sang it. It was very simple, but I had the good fortune to please Mozart. He took it and composed variations upon it, which were truly beautiful; and had the further kindness and condescension to play them wherever he had an opportunity.[7]

A version of this piece as a vocal trio for tenor, bass and soprano, orchestrated by Mozart for wind and bass survives in fragmentary form, K.532.

Mozart proceeded to give the aspiring composer advice as to how he should proceed with his career. Kelly continues:

Encouraged by his flattering approbation, I attempted several little airs, which I shewed him, and which he kindly approved of; so much indeed, that I determined to devote myself to the study of counterpoint, and consulted with him by whom I ought to be instructed. He said, "My good lad, you ask my advice, and I will give it to you candidly; had you studied composition when you were at Naples, and when your mind was not devoted to other pursuits, you would perhaps have done wisely; but now your profession of the stage must, and ought, to occupy all your attention, it would be an unwise measure to enter into a dry study. You may take my word for it, Nature has made you a melodist, and you would only disturb and perplex yourself. Reflect, 'a little knowledge is a dangerous thing'; should there be errors in what you write, you will find hundreds of musicians, in all parts of the world, capable of correcting them; therefore do not disturb your natural gift." "Melody is the essence of music", continued he; "I compare a good melodist to a fine racer, and counterpointists to hack post-horses; therefore be advised, let well alone, and remember the old Italian proverb—'Chi sa piu, men sa—Who knows most, knows least." The opinion of this great man made on me a lasting impression.[8]

Leaving aside the improbable words that Kelly put into Mozart's mouth when dictating his *Reminiscences* so many years later, the advice was very sound. Kelly remained no more than a melodist when, at the end of the century, he was employed in the unlikely role of resident composer to Drury Lane Theatre.

1786 was the year of Mozart's masterpiece, *Le nozze di Figaro*. Kelly gives a fascinating background to the production.[9] He says that early in that year there were three operas nearly ready for presentation at the same time, and that there was great competition among the composers who should get the prestige of being first. One was by Vicenzo Righini (1756–1812), director of the Italian opera, the second was by Antonio Salieri, and the third by Mozart, who had chosen Beaumarchais' highly controversial French comedy *Le mariage de Figaro* to be made into an Italian opera "which was done with great ability by Da Ponte". Kelly says, "Mozart was as touchy as gunpowder, and swore he would put the score of his opera into the fire if it was not pro-

duced first". The reason for Mozart's anxiety was that his future employment by the Emperor depended on his ability to compose opera buffa, now
demanded by the Viennese audiences. Kelly continues:

*Everyone of the opera company took part in the contest. I alone was a stickler
for Mozart, and naturally enough, for he had a claim on my warmest wishes,
from my adoration of his powerful genius, and the debt of gratitude I owed
him for many personal favours.*

The matter was resolved by Emperor Joseph, who issued a command for
Mozart's *Le nozze di Figaro* to be instantly put into rehearsal. Although regarded by the nobility as seditious and to be suppressed, the anti-aristo-
cratic tone of the opera was, in fact, much in keeping with the emperor's
firm views on state reform, which helps to explain why it received the royal
favour. Kelly says of the first performance:

*It was allowed that never was a stronger cast. I have seen it performed at dif-
ferent periods in other countries, and well too, but no more to compare with its
original performance than light is to darkness. All the original performers had
the advantage of the instruction of the composer, who transfused into their
minds his inspired meaning. I never shall forget his little animated countenance,
when lighted up with the glowing rays of genius;—it is impossible to describe
it, as it would be to paint sun-beams. . . . I remember at the first rehearsal of the
full band, Mozart was on the stage with his crimson pelisse and gold-laced
cocked hat, giving the time of the music to the orchestra. Figaro's song, 'Non
piu andrai, farfallone amoroso', Bennuci gave, with the greatest animation,
and power of voice.*

 *I was standing close to Mozart, who, sotto voce, was repeating, Bravo! Bravo!
Bennuci; and when Bennuci came to the fine passage, 'Cherubino, alla vittoria,
alla gloria militar', which he gave out with Stentorian lungs, the effect was ele-
ctricity itself, for the whole of the performers on the stage, and those in the orchestra, as if actuated by one feeling of delight, vociferated Bravo! Bravo!
Maestro. Viva, viva, grande Mozart. Those in the orchestra I thought would
never have ceased applauding, by beating the bows of their violins against the
music desks. The little man acknowledged, by repeated obeisances, his thanks for
the distinguished mark of enthusiastic applause bestowed upon him.*

Kelly, who was sometimes referred to in the cast as "O'Chelley", took the two minor parts of Don Basilio, the music master, and Don Curzio, the lawyer. He claims that he prevailed upon Mozart to allow him to portray the latter as a stuttering old man to enhance the comic effect, although it must be said that he rather overemphasises the importance of his roles.

It was always Kelly's ambition to savour the Viennese musical scene as much as possible, and he was gratified to be admitted to the *conversazioni* and musical parties given by Niccolo Martinez, the elderly master of ceremonies to the Papal Nuncio in Vienna, and his learned sister. The celebrated librettist, Metastasio, had lived with them all his long time in the city until his death and Mozart was a frequent attender of their parties. At one of them Kelly was also introduced to a visitor from England, Mrs Piozzi, a friend of Dr Johnson, and he says that it was his good fortune, on the same evening, to be in the company with the favourites of Metastasio and Dr Johnson, and last, not least, with Mozart himself.

One of several well-known musical figures residing in Vienna was court composer Cristoph von Gluck (1714–87), then in his seventy-second year. The emperor wished to have two of Gluck's operas produced. The first was to be *Iphigenie en Tauride*. Kelly, chosen to sing the part of Pylades, was coached in the role by Gluck himself. He says that the maestro attended the rehearsals, wearing his powdered wig and carrying a gold-headed cane. One morning after he had been receiving tuition, Gluck said, "Follow me upstairs, sir, and I will introduce you to one who, all my life, I have made my study and endeavoured to imitate". Kelly continues,

I followed him into his bedroom and opposite to the head of the bed saw a full-length picture of Handel in a rich frame. "There, sir," said he, "is the portrait of the inspired master of our art; when I open my eyes in the morning, I look upon him with reverential awe, and acknowledge him as such, and the highest praise is due to your country for having distinguished and cherished his gigantic genius".[10]

Gluck's relationship with the young Mozart was much more equivocal. There was a mutual respect for each other's achievements, but no real warmth had developed between the two composers. However, Kelly also made the acquaintance of one who was Mozart's hero, Joseph Haydn. He went out to Eisenstadt to see the great man, who had been Kapellmeister to the rich court of Prince Esterházy for many years. He spent three days with the maestro, the prince giving orders that his carriage should be used by

Haydn to drive his young guest all over the magnificent Esterházy estate. Kelly was to meet him again in the company of Mozart, in Vienna, and also much later, in 1792, during Haydn's stay in London, when he attended a dinner given in the composer's honour by his friend Stephen Storace.

Italian opera was performed three times a week and Kelly sang in most of the productions, which included Storace's two works commissioned by the emperor. After the performance of the second of these, *Gli equivoci*, at the end of 1786, Kelly petitioned the emperor for leave of absence to join the Storaces and Attwood on their return to England after the carnival in February. This was granted and that night Kelly says that he went gambling at the Redoutensaal but lost more than he could pay. He speaks of the generous nature of Nancy Storace who, unasked, insisted on paying his debt to avoid any embarrassment to his career on returning to England. When the time came for the departure from Vienna, Kelly said,

I went to take leave of the immortal Mozart and his charming wife and family; he gave me a letter to his father, Leopold Mozart, who was at the Court of Salzburg. I could hardly tear myself away from him, and, at parting, we both shed tears. Indeed, the memory of the many happy days which I passed at Vienna will never be effaced from my mind.[1]

Crowned with success, the British friends returned to England in March 1787, and Kelly saw London for the first time in his life. He was then twenty four years old, untried in England, but with a great European experience. He had a contract from Thomas Linley to sing at the Drury Lane Theatre, and his debut was on 20 April 1787 in *Lionel and Clarissa*, the opera in which he had made his first appearance at the age of sixteen in Dublin. This time music was added by Stephen Storace. It was soon after his arrival in London that he first met a former pupil of Thomas Linley, the lovely soprano Mrs Anna Crouch (1763–1805) who was also a member of the Drury Lane company. He stayed with her and her husband in the Crouch household in Suffolk Street, Pall Mall, where they entertained many luminaries including Sheridan and the Prince of Wales, both of whom became close friends of Kelly. When, in 1791, husband and wife separated, it appears that the ever eager prince briefly took Mrs Crouch to be his mistress before relinquishing her to Kelly, who formed a loving relationship with her which was to last until her death in 1805.

During the time of the French Revolution Kelly made several trips to

Paris, ostensibly to obtain new operatic material for Drury Lane. His visit in the summer of 1791 was never to be forgotten. He was there in the Tuilleries when Louis XVI and Marie Antoinette were returned as prisoners after their escape to Varennes, before being executed the following year:

I was quite close to the carriage when they dismounted; nothing could be more majestic than the conduct of the Queen, when Dupont (a member of the National Assembly), offered to hand her from the carriage; she waved her hand, and walked with a firm step into the palace, without accepting his aid. She was plainly dressed, and, I remember, wore a black bonnet, covered with dust.[12]

Kelly continued singing at Drury Lane, taking all the main male operatic roles including those written by his friend Stephen Storace. In 1793, when the rebuilt King's Theatre finally reassumed its place as the centre of Italian opera, Kelly and Storace were appointed as its joint managers, in addition to their work in English opera at Drury Lane, so that for a time Nancy Storace and Kelly sang at both theatres.

Following the death of Stephen Storace in 1796, Nancy left Drury Lane and in the following year departed abroad with her lover, John Braham. Probably because there was no one else suitable, Kelly then became resident composer at Drury Lane. Unable to orchestrate, his method of composition was to provide the melody from which others would then produce the score. It is not surprising that there were no major successes apart from his opera *Blue Beard* (1798), based upon the French opera of the same name he had seen in Paris. Feeling the need to diversify his income, in 1802 Kelly set up a music shop in Pall Mall near the King's Theatre. The shop also sold wine to the theatre clientele, leading his great friend and wit, Sheridan, to dub him "Composer of wines and importer of music".[13]

Three years later his beloved Mrs Crouch died, and on 5 September 1811 he appeared for the last time on the stage. That same day, with the failure of his music shop, he was declared bankrupt, a misfortune which he ascribed to the deficiencies of his business manager. Gradually his close friends died: Sheridan in 1816, and Nancy Storace in the following year. He continued to compose until 1820, claiming that, in all, he had written a total of sixty-two pieces. As he approached the age of sixty he became more and more incapacitated by gout, but found solace in being able to spend time in Brighton with his royal friend, now King George IV.

On 9th October 1826 Kelly died at Margate at age sixty four. His body was taken back to London and was buried in the church much associated with the theatre, St Paul's, Covent Garden.

When assessing Michael Kelly's career on the stage it is necessary to discount the overemphasis on his prowess as an actor related in the *Reminiscences*. Nevertheless, he was, by the standards of the day, a very successful tenor, and he is particularly notable as being the first on the English stage to sing without resorting to falsetto. It seems that until Kelly's time it was the practice of even the famous tenors such as Beard to sing falsetto in the high register, and this was accepted by audiences as a natural manner of singing. A contemporary wrote, "His compass was extraordinary. In vigorous passages he never cheated the ear with feeble wailings of falsetto, but sprung upon the ascending fifth with a sustained energy that electrified the audience".[14] His unfailing good humour, his Irish gift of conversation, and his profession allowed him to mix with many of the great figures of the late eighteenth century, all of whom he describes with verve, including his vivid portrait of Mozart, in his *Reminiscences*.

FIG. 9. Nancy Storace (1765–1817) as Euphrosyne in 'Comus' by Thomas Arne. Engraving by Condé after a painting by Samuel de Wilde, 1791. © *The Trustees of the British Museum*.

NANCY STORACE

O
N 1ST MAY 1786, AT THE BURGTHEATER IN VIENNA, MOZART CONDUCTED the première of *Le nozze di Figaro*. In this marvellous opera Mozart created the central role of Susanna for one of his close women friends, a twenty-year-old English soprano, Ann Selina Storace, who, for the last three years, had reigned as the darling of the Viennese opera. A contemporary critic wrote,

Storace, the beautiful singer, enchanted eye, ear, and soul.—Mozart directed the orchestra, playing his fortepiano; but the joy which this music causes is so far removed from all sensuality that one cannot speak of it. Where could words be found that are worthy to describe such a joy?[1]

Ann Selina (Nancy) Storace was the second child of an Italian double-bass player, Stephen Storace, who had settled in England and had married Elizabeth Trusler of Bath. It was probably through her that the Storace family became acquainted with the Linleys, and after Sheridan married Elizabeth Linley the newlywed couple made their first home with the Storaces in London. Nancy was born in Marylebone on 27th October 1765 and was the sister of the composer Stephen Storace the younger. Under the tuition of her father, Nancy showed her singing ability from a very early age. At age seven she appeared in public at concerts in Southampton and then at Salisbury, where she sang, accompanied by her father and ten-year-old brother as instrumentalists. A report in the *Salisbury Journal* says, "We must not omit to do justice to the merits of Miss Storace who sung several songs with great spirit and judgment and shewed uncommon signs of an early genius to music".[2]

Realising her talent, her father arranged for her to have further teaching by the well-known male soprano and composer, Venanzio Rauzzini (1746–1810), who had recently settled in England. Mozart had previously written for him the title role of his opera *Lucio Silla* and the beautiful solo motet 'Exultate, jubilate'. In London, Rauzzini performed at the King's Theatre, and on 29th December 1776, his eleven-year-old protégée Nancy

Storace appeared there for her first operatic role as Cupid in *L'ali d'amore*, composed by Rauzzini.

In December 1778 Nancy travelled with her parents to Naples to join her brother Stephen who was studying music there. She went on to stay in Europe for over eight years, during which time she succeeded, at an improbably early age, in singing at all the major Italian opera houses. By the time she was seventeen she had reached the pinnacle of her profession and was performing at La Scala in Milan. In winter 1782 Michael Kelly found her singing at the theatre of San Samuele in Venice, where he says she drew overflowing houses and was showered with gifts of all kinds.

Meanwhile, in Vienna, the dominant opera had been German, but by 1783 it was in disarray. Emperor Joseph, acting in his self assumed role of theatre director, and in deference to the tastes of the opera-loving public, resolved to establish a first-class Italian opera company. He offered tempting salaries to obtain the services of top male Italian singers such as Francesco Benucci and Stefano Mandini. Through his ambassador in Venice, Count Giacomo Durazzo, the emperor sought out Nancy Storace, the then-famous eighteen-year-old English soprano, to be prima donna.

Nancy arrived in Vienna from her triumphs in Venice in spring 1783, chaperoned by her mother. Her first appearance was in the opera *La scuola degli gelosi*, by the music director of the new company, Antonio Salieri. Count Zinzendorf, an ardent theatre-goer, who had more of an eye for the prima donna than an ear for her vocal performance, wrote in his diary on 22nd April 1783, "Mlle Storace the Englishwoman, a pretty, voluptuous figure, beautiful neck, and good as a Bohemian girl. . . . The audience was greatly pleased".[3] On 13th August, Nancy sang the role of Rosina in the first Viennese production of Paisiello's enormously successful *Il barbiere di Siviglia*. The Emperor was delighted with his company's performance and on the following day he wrote "As for their acting, they acquitted themselves even better than was hoped, above all Benucci. . . . La Storace sang an aria cantabile very well".[4]

As can be imagined, Mozart witnessed the arrival of the new opera buffa company with great interest. He wrote to his father on 7th May,

Well, the Italian opera buffa has started again here and is very popular. The buffo is particularly good—his name is Benucci. . . . Our poet here is a now a certain Abbate da Ponte. He has an enormous amount to do in revising pieces for the theatre and he has to write per obbligo an entirely new libretto for Salieri, which will take him two months. He has promised after that to write a new libretto for me. . . . I should dearly love to show what I can do in Italian opera![5]

It seems that da Ponte kept his promise because in a letter dated the 5th July, Mozart states that he had just received a libretto from an "Italian poet" and it is believed that it was for his new comic opera *Il sposo deluso*. Mozart now set about composing the music. It was to have an imposing caste from the Italian company, and for the leading buffa role he chose Nancy Storace, with whom he had recently become acquainted. The overture, two arias, a trio and a quartet were written for *Il sposo deluso*, but by the end of the year Mozart had abandoned the work as impracticable. It is, however, noteworthy that in his entry of the cast list of the projected opera Mozart refers to Nancy as Signora Fischer whereas only a few months earlier, on 2nd July, he has called her Mlle Storace.

Soon after her arrival in Vienna in 1783, Nancy met an English violinist and composer, Dr John Abraham Fisher (1744–1806). He was more than twice her age but by the autumn they were married. It is stated by Kelly that Fisher ingratiated himself with Nancy's mother by drinking endless cups of tea with her. The wedding was attended by a large number of the English aristocracy who were in Vienna. Lord Mount-Edgcumbe led her to the altar, and the British ambassador, Sir Robert Keith, gave the wedding dinner. Fisher may have been an eminent doctor of music but, by all accounts, he seems to have been a most unprepossessing character. He is referred to by Kelly as "a very ugly Christian" and "an inordinate prattler".[6] Unsurprisingly, within a few months the incongruous marriage was at an end. Stories that Fisher was guilty of striking his wife during fits of temper reached the ears of the Emperor Joseph who, it is said, was himself more than partial to Nancy and he took the drastic step of banishing the doctor from Vienna. Nancy never saw him again, and, subsequently, she never acknowledged the fact that she had ever been married to him.

Nancy continued to sing in many leading roles with the Italian opera company, and in 1784 she was joined by Michael Kelly, whom she first met in Leghorn three years previously. They sang together at Kelly's Viennese debut in Paisiello's *Il re Teodoro in Venezia* on 23rd August 1784. Mozart attended this first performance but he was taken severely ill with what appears to have been a stomach complaint.[7]

In May 1786 Mozart's sequel to Paisiello's *Il barbiere di Siviglia* was premiered. While at first it seemed natural that in *Le nozze di Figaro* Nancy would again sing the role of Rosina, the character had now become a fine countess, and Nancy's temperament was far more in keeping with that of the pert, saucy, Susanna. Mozart wrote the part with his close knowledge of Nancy Storace very much in mind. Michael Kelly says of this:

I called on him [Mozart] one evening; he said to me, "I have just finished a little duet for my opera, you shall hear it." He sat down to the piano, and we sang it. I was delighted with it, and the musical world will give me credit for being so, when I mention the duet, sung by Count Almaviva and Susanna, 'Crudel! perche finora farmi languire cosi.' A more delicious morceau never was penned by man.[8]

Nancy Storace was now the highest paid singer in Vienna, and it was in the role of the soubrette in comic opera that she excelled. Not for her were the grand heroines of opera seria. More than her voice, it was her vivacious, generous personality which drew so many male admirers, including the Emperor Joseph, to this short, plumpish, English girl. An anecdote from Kelly provides information about her closeness to the emperor. He tells of the occasion when, as members of the Italian opera company, splendid facilities were provided for them to relax in the surroundings of the imperial summer palace at Laxenburg, outside Vienna, and that when Nancy felt thirsty she casually asked Joseph to obtain a glass of water for her.

At this time Vienna was favoured by a large number of resident young English aristocracy who regularly met in a house in the Graben, where they formed a club at which they dined and drank extensively. They also frequented that centre of social activity in the city, the Redoutensaal, where there was dancing and gambling. Among these young bloods was twenty-year-old William, Lord Barnard (1766–1842), later Duke of Cleveland, who was great-great-grandson of Charles II and Lady Castlemaine. Like other men, Lord Barnard laid siege to the affections of Nancy Storace, as his diary, written in French, testifies. At the beginning of 1787 he writes:

January 20th.—I spent the evening with Madame Storace. January 21st.—I supped with La Storace. I took her to the Ridotto (Redoutensaal) where we stayed until 4 a.m. January 24th.—I went to La Storace's house. I supped at her house. February 3rd.—I gave a ball at my house for La Storace. The weather was very fine and warm. February 4th.—I went with La Storace to the Ridotto. February 10th.—I supped with La Storace. February 23rd.—At the concert of Madame Storace who supped with me.[9]

The following day Lord Barnard departed from Vienna, but not from Nancy's life.

By this time it seems probable that Mozart also was enamoured of his first Susanna. Much to his undoubted dismay, she had already signalled her intention of returning to London with the other members of Mozart's English circle. The date of her farewell concert at the Karntnerthor theatre was 23rd February. On this sad occasion she sang a lovely scena and aria, written specially for her by Mozart, 'Ch'io mi scordi di te . . . Non temer, amato bene', K.505, and the obbligato piano was played by Mozart himself. The words which Nancy sang had a particular poignancy: "Shall I ever forget you, don't be afraid my beloved, my heart will be ever yours". In his own thematic catalogue, Mozart enters it, touchingly, as "Für M'selle Storace und mich," and the autograph reads "Composto per La Sig^{ra} Storace dal suo servo ed amico W. A. Mozart, Vienna li 26 di dec^{bre} 1786." Einstein calls it a declaration of love in music.[10]

A more discordant note was struck by a critic of the concert:

But artistic Talent, what canst thou expect of thy fatherland, where people fight to hear a few arias sung at a bad concert by the arrogant foreigner Storace, whose Talent for art equals that for impertinence, while thy Mozart, so excellent an artist, is not even paid as much for a good concert as will cover his costs for it.[11]

This correspondent was referring to the huge sum received by Nancy Storace for this concert, reputedly to be over four thousand gulden.

At the end of February 1787, in the company of her mother, her brother, Michael Kelly, Thomas Attwood and her lapdog, she left Vienna and Mozart, vowing to arrange for him to come to London. They took with them the letter of introduction from Mozart to visit his father in Salzburg, where he was now living alone, not in the best of health. Kelly says that on the morning after their arrival in Salzburg he went to see Leopold:

I found him a pleasing intelligent little man; he called upon Signora Storace, and offered to be our guide to everything worth noticing; he was, as I have mentioned, in the service of the reigning Sovereign, the Archbishop, who, was passionately fond of music. . . . The Archbishop sent one of his attendants to invite Signora Storace and her party to hear a concert at his palace; we felt ourselves highly honoured and, of course, went. The Archbishop was a very fine-looking man, particularly gallant and attentive towards the ladies, of whom there was a splendid show; it was conceived that he was very partial to the English, and English manners.[12]

This was the Archbishop who had so violently disagreed with Leopold's son that his chamberlain had literally kicked him out of his court.

Leopold, in a letter to his daughter Nannerl, dated 1st March 1787, gives more details of his meeting with his son's English friends:

At halfpast six o'clock on Monday evening I received from Madame Storace, the Vienna opera singer, a note saying that she had arrived at the Trinkstube. I found her mother with her, who is an Englishwoman (the daughter was born in England), the Vienna opera tenor O'Kelly, who is an Englishman by birth, her brother Maestro Storace, and a little Englishman called Attwood who was sent to Vienna two years ago for the sole purpose of taking lessons from your brother. As Madame Storace had a letter of introduction from Countess Guntacker Colloredo, the Archbishop was obliged to hear her sing and to give her a handsome present. After a year's stay in London she is returning to the Vienna opera [she never did return]. *I galloped round the town with them on Tuesday from ten to two in order to show them a few sights. We lunched at two o'clock. In the evening she sang three arias and they left for Munich at midnight. They had two carriages, each with four post-horses. A servant rode in advance as courier to arrange the changing of eight horses. Goodness, what baggage they had! This journey must have cost them a fortune.*[13]

Three months later Leopold was dead.

The party reached Munich and, not surprisingly, at their inn was none other than Lord Barnard, who had arrived there from Vienna. He invited them to dine with him, and then they continued their journey in his company, with Nancy often riding in his carriage. Travelling by way of Paris, where they went to see Grétry's opera, *Richard Coeur de Lion*, they crossed the channel from Boulogne to Dover, arriving in London in the middle of March.

In spite of her great reputation on the continent, Nancy Storace had to contend with the ingrained antagonism of the Italian opera company to English singers. Nevertheless, she returned to the King's Theatre in the Haymarket at which she had last appeared at age thirteen. Her first performance was in Paisiello's *Schiavi per amore* on 24th April 1787. The Prince of Wales, with whom she later became very well acquainted, was in the audience.

Lord Barnard was a member of the society which thronged round the prince, as his diary shows. But on his return to London, his feeling for the opera singer was fast fading, and the name of the aristocratic Lady Katherine Powlett, daughter of the Duke of Bolton, now appears. He attended a benefit concert for Nancy on 24th May, but only two weeks later came the last occasion of their meeting. On 6th June, obviously a hectic day for him, he writes in his diary, "I was at Bolton House all afternoon. I dined with Mademoiselle Storace. I went to Bolton House".[14] Three months later Lord Barnard and Lady Katherine were married.

During early summer 1787 the Handel Commemoration Festival was held in Westminster Abbey, and for a grand performance of *Messiah*, the audience was graced by the presence of the king and queen, who were great admirers of Handel. Among the many well-known soloists who took part was Nancy Storace, although it must be said that singing in *Messiah* was not her usual métier. Nevertheless, Lord Mount-Edgcumbe, while commenting on her general inappropriateness for opera seria, said that she was magnificent in oratorio in Westminster Abbey, since in that space the harsh part of her voice was lost while its power and clearness filled the whole of it. In her more accustomed roles of comic opera, Nancy continued singing for the King's Theatre, in Paisello's *Il re Teodoro in Venezia*, followed later by her brother's only Italian opera for this theatre, *La cameriera astuta*.

It is clear that the Storaces brought back with them from Vienna a copy of the full score of *Le nozze di Figaro* with the probable intention of staging a performance, but for technical reasons it was then not possible to produce the whole opera for the London stage. Nevertheless, after her return, Nancy used every opportunity to introduce Mozart's arias to London audiences when they were unknown in England. In May 1789 Giuseppe Gazzaniga's opera *La vendemmia* was given at the King's Theatre and, following the practice at the time, it contained additional music from several other composers, including Mozart. Nancy Storace, the first Susanna, and Francesco Bennuci, the first Figaro, sang the duet 'Crudel! perche finora' from *Le nozze di Figaro*, to much acclaim by the critics.

A second opportunity arose the following year when on 27th February the pasticcio opera *La villanella rapita* was produced. A notice in *The Public Advertiser* states, "A new comic opera was last night produced. . . . The music of it is evidently a melange though announced as the composition of Bianchi and Hogart."[15] The latter should read "Mozart" and it was notable for the fact that Nancy Storace sang Susanna's aria 'Deh veni non tardar' from *Figaro* and 'Batti, batti' from *Don Giovanni*.[16] At this time *Don Gio-*

vanni had not yet been published in England so that a copy must have been sent to Nancy by Mozart himself. In June 1789 she gave a benefit performance for which she chose one of her triumphs from Vienna, the role of Rosina in *Il barbiere di Siviglia*, with Kelly as Count Almaviva. A few days later the King's Theatre was burnt down and she turned her attention to English opera by joining Michael Kelly at Drury Lane, where her brother was now resident composer and music director under the management of Richard Brinsley Sheridan. The partnership of brother and sister was displayed for the first time in November of that year, with Stephen Storace's *Haunted Tower*. This was followed by all his subsequent works.

March 1796 saw Stephen Storace's untimely death. Nancy sang in his last opera, *Mahmoud*, with a young, very promising tenor, John Braham (1774–1856), who was making his first appearance in London. Like Nancy, Braham had been taught by the great Venanzio Rauzzini, now resident in Bath, and had already been selected by Stephen Storace for *Mahmoud* before the composer's death. His meeting with Nancy became the start of a liaison which lasted twenty years. They became lovers and the following year they left England for an extended tour of the Continent during which, over a period of five years, they sang together in France, Italy and Germany. They returned in 1802, and on 3rd May their son, John Spencer, was born.[17]

The partnership at Drury Lane continued until Nancy retired in May 1808, when she was still only forty two. Her last performance was in one of her brother's greatest successes, *No Song, No Supper*. Never a great beauty, she had become rather stout and coarse in appearance and her voice was finished. The years of singing from a preternaturally early age had taken its toll. The relationship with the very successful tenor, John Braham, who was nine years her junior, was bound to suffer, and in 1816 the liaison came to an end with much distress on Nancy's part.

She went to live with her aged mother in Herne Hill, Dulwich, and in the following year she died. Kelly tells us that on the day before her death she dined with him at his house in Great Russell Street, Covent Garden:

In the course of the evening she was all at once taken with a shivering fit and appeared very ill. When her carriage came to take her home, Mr Savory [a fellow guest] requested her to be bled, and to send for Dr Hooper. On the following day Dr Hooper went to her country house at Herne Hill and advised her by all means to be bled, but she would not consent because it was Friday; thus, in fact, she sacrificed herself to superstition.[18]

It is stated by her mother that she searched her daughter's bureau after her death, looking for her will, and it contained a number of important papers under lock and key. Among these, it is believed, there was the correspondence which Nancy maintained with Mozart after her return to England. Unfortunately, it has never come to light.

After this interval of time it is difficult to assess the real nature of Nancy Storace's voice. On her return to London in 1787 Charles Burney, as always, gave his views:

But though a lively and intelligent actress and an excellent performer in comic operas, her voice, in spite of all her care, does not favour her ambition to appear as a serious singer. There is a certain crack and roughness which, though it fortifies the humour and effects of a comic song in scenes where laughing, scolding, crying, or quarrelling is necessary; yet in airs of tenderness, sorrow, or supplication there is always reason to lament the deficiency of natural sweetness, where art and pains are not wanting.[19]

There is in fact no evidence that Nancy held any ambitions for opera seria and Burney was seldom satisfied with English singers of his beloved Italian opera. It is likely that, in the eighteenth century, critical opinion was very different from that of today, but simply judged from the size of the audiences she was able to attract in the great musical centres of Europe and in London, Nancy Storace was a phenomenally successful artist. According to some contemporary critics her retirement came not before time, but the promotion of singers at the early age experienced by Nancy Storace and others of that era would not, nowadays, be regarded as conducive to a long vocal career. Her obituary in the *Gentlemen's Magazine* read:

At Herne Hill, near Dulwich, aged 49 [actually 51], Signora Storace, sister of Stephen Storace, the eminent composer. Of her professional talents as a singer and as an actress it is unnecessary to say anything; they were the delight and the admiration of the publick; and certainly she was altogether unrivalled in her particular line. She was not handsome, nor feminine in her person; but one of the most accomplished and agreeable women of her age—fascinating everyone by her habitual good humour, her lively and intelligent conversation and her open and ingenuous character.[20]

And among the many men she fascinated was Mozart.

FIG. 10. Stephen Storace (1762–96). Engraving from title page of 'Mahmoud' and 'The Iron Chest', his last two operas. *By Permission of the British Library: Music Library, E.115.a (1).*

❧ CHAPTER XIII ❧
STEPHEN STORACE

IT IS A SAD COINCIDENCE THAT TWO OF MOZART'S CLOSE FRIENDS, EITHER of whom could have become the most important English composer of the late eighteen century, died young. The first was Thomas Linley, and the second was Stephen Storace.

Born on 4th April 1762, Stephen Storace was the elder brother of Nancy. Their father, Stephen Storace senior, was for a time, music director of the Marylebone pleasure gardens. Under his tuition the boy became a good violinist, but in 1776, realising the lack of first-class music teaching in England, he decided to send his son to Italy to study with Giacomo Insanguine (1728–95), organist and master in composition at the conservatorio, San Onofrio, in Naples. Stephen junior was then fourteen years old and was lodged with his uncle, who was a bishop in the city. His father's attempts to launch him on a musical career were, initially, not very promising. While he was in Naples, Stephen became friendly with the Welsh landscape painter Thomas Jones (1742–1803). In his memoirs Jones describes the boy as "a giddy and thoughtless fellow who apply'd very little to his Musical Studies and being tired of the restraints he felt under his Uncle's roof, lived entirely with the English, and as he was fond of Drawing, was almost always of our parties".[1]

Some of the disaffection with music felt by Stephen may have been due to the conditions at San Onofrio. The conservatorio had about ninety boys from eight to twenty years old. In the past it had produced many famous operatic composers, such as Jommelli and Piccinni, but it seems that it was now in decline. Charles Burney had visited San Onofrio six years previously and wrote,

These celebrated seminaries which have heretofore produced so many great professors seem at present but low in genius, but perhaps these institutions, like others, are subject to fluctuations, and after some time, like their neighbour Mount Vesuvius, they will blaze again with new vigour.[2]

It appeared that after Stephen had spent three years in Naples, San

Onofrio had still not yet "blazed" and his parents arrived, with his sister Nancy, to remove him from the conservatorio. By 1780 Stephen was back in England, leaving his sister, chaperoned by her mother, to pursue her rise to fame in Italy. For a time he lived in Bath and, still not certain about pursuing a musical career, he considered becoming a painter. However, his mood obviously changed because in 1782 there appeared his first published musical compositions, eight canzonettas—songs with piano and harp accompaniment. One of these was a setting of Thomas Gray's famous poem 'Elegy in a Country Churchyard'. The lament-like music is very appropriate for the fine words and it makes a most worthy composition.

In 1781 Stephen returned to Italy and joined his sister in Leghorn, where she was then singing as prima donna. It was here that the Storaces first encountered that young, garrulous Irishman, Michael Kelly, who gives a graphic description of how their friendship first began. He had a fair complexion and long flowing hair, and as he came ashore at Leghorn, dressed in a Sicilian cloak, he heard Nancy say to Stephen, laughingly in English, not thinking she would be understood by the object of her amusement, "Look at that girl dressed in boy's clothes!" To which Kelly replied, much to her surprise, "You are mistaken, Miss; I am a very proper he animal, and quite at your service".[3] They remained friends for the rest of their lives. Stephen's experiences in Italy must have further stimulated his musical talent because after his return to England in 1784 he published three instrumental compositions, two quintets in B flat and D major as well as a sextet.

Meanwhile, in Vienna, Nancy had become the star of the Italian opera company and a great favourite of Emperor Joseph II. It seems likely that she showed him copies of her brother's chamber works and such was her influence that Stephen, as yet completely untried in theatre music, was commissioned by the emperor to write an opera.

He was in Vienna for the première of this work, the comic opera *Gli sposi malcontenti*, on 1st June 1785, which was performed in the presence of the emperor and an English visitor, the young Duke of York. Michael Kelly and Nancy sang the leading roles. But halfway through the first act disaster struck when Nancy suddenly lost her voice. Kelly says,

the loss of the first female singer, who was a great and deserved favourite, was to the composer, her brother, a severe blow. I never shall forget her despair and disappointment, but she was not then prepared for the extent of her misfortune, for she did not recover her voice sufficiently to appear on the stage for five months.[4]

Her recovery, in fact, took place in September and Mozart contributed to the writing of a cantata, 'Per la ricuperata salute di Ophelia', to celebrate Nancy's return. The work was published, but it is now lost. The title refers to the role of Ophelia which Nancy was then rehearsing for Salieri's new opera *La grotta di Trefonio*. In spite of this setback, *Gli sposi malcontenti* subsequently proved to be a great success, resulting in a further commission by the emperor.

Storace's second opera, *Gli equivoci*, had a libretto by no less than Lorenzo da Ponte, whose last work had been *Le nozze di Figaro*. By Stephen's choice it was based on Shakespeare's *Comedy of Errors*, and it was probably the first time that a Shakespeare play had been used as the subject of an opera. The first performance was on 27th December 1786, with Kelly as one of the twins and Nancy in the first female role. It is of considerable length, and again, it proved to be a great success, playing at many of the opera houses of Europe for several years.

What is so surprising about both Storace's Viennese operas is the excellent quality of the music, as his published record had hitherto been so slim. They are decidedly Mozartian in style and it has been thought, probably correctly, that Storace not only received lessons in composition from Mozart but that the master added his own touches to the scores, such is their sophistication.[5]

By this time Mozart was a close friend of both Storaces, as well as Kelly, who gives a fascinating glimpse of their relationships. He says that he was present on one occasion when Stephen gave a party for his friends at his house. A quartet played. He lists the members as Haydn, first violin; Dittersdorf (in his time a greatly renowned composer), second violin; Vanhal (also a well-known composer), cello; Mozart, viola. Of this most distinguished quartet Kelly writes,

Not one of them excelled on the instrument he played, but there was a little science among them, which I dare say will be acknowledged when I name them! . . . After the musical feast was over we sat down to an excellent supper and became joyous in the extreme.[6]

Early in 1787 Stephen prepared to return to London with his sister and other English friends, but four days before their departure Kelly tells us of an incident that threatened to delay their arrangements. It was the time of the Vienna carnival and, at one of the many balls which were given, Stephen became somewhat confused after drinking too much champagne. Nancy was dancing with an officer but tripped and fell to the ground. Stephen, thinking that his sister had been insulted, attacked the officer. Whereupon, the police were called and he was thrown into gaol. The next morning Kelly made it his business to see the emperor who laughed and said "I am very sorry for Storace, for he is a man of great talent; but I regret to observe that some of your English gentry who travel, appear to be much altered from what they used to be".[7] The emperor then gave instructions for Stephen to be released. This account is largely confirmed in a letter Stephen Storace himself wrote from gaol on the following day, 21st February, to J. Serres, a friend in London. The letter also tells of the unseemly behaviour of many young English aristocrats at this time:

you must know that there never perhaps was so hard: a going sett [sic] of English in any one town out of England—as are at present in Vienna—we have lived these last six weeks almost in one continual scene of riot—among ourselves—as long as it remained so, nobody could find fault—but lately some of our youths—high charged with the juice of French grapes—have made occasional sallies—and exposed themselves to the natives especially at the Ridotta's or Masquerades.[8]

Storace's own version of events differs slightly from that of Kelly in that Nancy's dancing partner was in fact Lord Barnard, and it was he who was insulted by the officer with whom Storace quarrelled. But the behaviour of the English in Vienna at this time explains why Storace was arrested so quickly, and also the emperor's comments.

A few days after his release from gaol, Stephen Storace departed from Vienna in the company of the three other English travellers. He finally reached London on 18th March 1787. The evening of their arrival Storace went with Kelly to the home of his friend, Thomas Linley, in the Strand. Linley was by now director of music at Drury Lane, but he had never really recovered from the devastating blow of the death of his son, Tom. With him were his daughters, the famous Linley sisters, Elizabeth and Mary, the latter already dying of tuberculosis. It was Elizabeth who asked the two visitors to go that evening to Drury Lane Theatre to give her their impression of the opera she had adapted for the English stage, *Richard Coeur de Lion*, by the French composer Grétry. Together with the other English travellers, Kelly and Stephen Storace had seen its performance in Paris four days previously, but were decidedly unimpressed with the London version since, in the absence of a capable tenor, the part of Richard was taken by the actor John Kemble.

Kelly had a contract to appear at Drury Lane, where the acquisition of a first-class tenor was greeted with great relief. But in spite of their friendship with Linley, the Storaces thought that their place would naturally be the King's Theatre in the Haymarket, where their extensive experience of Italian opera would be welcomed. But they had not reckoned with the longstanding antagonism which that company had always shown to non-Italian artists and composers, and it was with some difficulty that they were accepted. In July of that year Stephen Storace was writing to Sir Robert Keith, British ambassador in Vienna:

My sister's success in London upon the whole has been much as we could expect, though she has had great opposition from the Italians, who consider it as an infringement on their rights that any person should be able to sing that was not born in Italy.[9]

In the event, Stephen was invited to write a new comic opera for the King's Theatre. His first opera in England, *La cameriera astuta*, was performed on 4th March 1788. It was not a success and was said by the critics to be too much of the "German" style, probably because it was too Mozartian. He was not asked again to write for the Italian company.

Later in 1788 Storace transferred to English opera at Drury Lane and for the next eight years he was extremely prolific, producing seven full-length and eight short operas. *The Haunted Tower* (1789) signalled his success as an operatic composer in London, and a short opera, *No Song, No Supper*, proved to be remarkably popular, with performances continuing into the next century. The next work, *The Siege of Belgrade* (1791), was based on Martin y Soler's *Una cosa rara* and is notable for the fact that the overture incorporates Mozart's famous rondo *alla turca* to introduce a chorus of Turks. There followed, in November 1792, Storace's best English opera, *The Pirates*, which was set in Naples, a location familiar to the composer. His artistic skills, dating from his youth, are seen in the scenery and title page of the vocal score, which were based upon his sketches of Naples.

The next full length opera, *The Cherokee* (1794), featuring a Red Indian chorus, reflected England's new found interest in the North American Indian. This was the first time that the Wild West had been the subject of opera.

During his stay in Vienna, the only Mozart opera which Storace would have seen was *Le nozze di Figaro*. It is therefore not surprising that echoes of *Figaro* are seen in several of his operas. Unfortunately, while much of Storace's surviving music is of fine quality, his librettists are often inferior to the task, and the operas are therefore not generally to modern taste. It is perhaps not surprising that the one which can most bear a modern revival is *Gli equivoci*, with a libretto by da Ponte.

During 1787–89 Storace published a large collection of music for the harpsichord or piano, which included three trios of his own composition, but much had been collected in Vienna from various sources. Among these was Mozart's Piano Quartet in E flat, K.493, which had only recently appeared in Vienna, the Rondo for Piano Solo in F, K.494, and the very first edition of the Piano Trio in G, K.564. Since this work was quite new, and had not previously been published anywhere, it must have been sent to Stephen Storace by Mozart himself.

It was at this time in 1788 that Stephen married Ann Hall, the daughter of the engraver, John Hall, who was responsible for the decoration of his published collection. They had a son, Brinsley, but he died at age nineteen.

Two vocal compositions of Storace which appeared following the execution of Marie Antoinette and Louis XVI in 1793 are of interest. One is entitled 'Captivity, a Ballad supposed to be sung by the Unfortunate Marie Antoinette, during her Imprisonment in the Temple' and this was followed by 'A Lamentation of Marie Antoinette, late Queen of France, on the Morning of her Execution'. These songs indicate Storace's depth of feeling about an event which touched him personally in view of his previous close contacts in Vienna with Marie Antoinette's brother, the emperor.

The last two of Storace's operas were tinged with sadness. In March 1796, while working on his penultimate work, *The Iron Chest*, he became very ill with pains in the joints and fever and had to be carried to the theatre for the first rehearsal in a sedan chair, wrapped in blankets. He returned to bed at his home in Percy Street, Tottenham Court Road, never to arise again. Kelly was very distressed and tells of his last meeting with the friend he first met on the quay at Leghorn fifteen years earlier:

I called upon him the night of the day which had been the rehearsal: he sent for me to his bedside, and pressing my hand he said "My dear Mick, I have tried to finish your song, but find myself unable to accomplish it. I must be ill indeed when I can't write for you, who have given so much energy to my compositions".[10]

On 19th March, one week after the first performance of *The Iron Chest*, Stephen Storace died at age thirty three. He was buried in the parish church of St Marylebone High Street, now demolished. His last opera, *Mahmoud*, was unfinished at his death and was completed by his sister and Kelly. It was produced on 30th April of the same year and all the profits were given for the benefit of Storace's widow and child.

Much of Storace's work has been lost because of Sheridan's policy of not publishing the librettos for fear they would be pirated, and because of the burning of the theatre, which destroyed the scores. As Kelly says in his memoirs when describing the Drury Lane fire of 1809, "I had not only the poignant grief of beholding the magnificent structure burning with merciless fury, but of knowing that all the scores of the operas which I had composed for the theatre, the labour of years, were then consuming".[11] Nevertheless, the amount of his work which does remain marks Stephen Storace as being one of the most significant figures of English music in the late eighteenth century, and it was unfortunate for the development of music in this country that both he and the younger Linley should have died at such an early age. It is clear that Storace completely revolutionised ideas on the making of an opera which had, hitherto, held sway in the English theatre. In composition, the old relationship between librettist and composer was reversed, so that the words were adapted to the music instead of the author of the words exerting the dominant role, as was the usual practice. An article on Storace in the *Thespian Dictionary* of 1802 states,

It must, however, be remarked, that the words [of his librettos] *were chiefly adapted to the music: indeed, Mr Storace openly declared in a music-sellers shop in Cheapside (then Longman & Broderip's) that it was impossible for any author to produce a good opera, without previously consulting his intended composer, for, added he, the songs must be introduced as he pleases, and the words (which are a secondary consideration) be written agreeably to his directions.*[12]

He had imbibed these concepts from his association with Mozart who, writing to his father in 1781, expressed the philosophy which Storace adopted:

I should say that in an opera the poetry must be altogether the obedient daughter of the music. . . . Why, an opera is sure of success when the plot is well worked out, the words written for the music, and not shoved in here and there to suit some miserable rhyme.[13]

When it came to the staging of an opera, Storace insisted on action during the music so that in place of ensembles where the protagonists stood stiffly in line to sing to the audience, as was the fashion, they moved freely, acting their parts while singing. In these ideas he was, of course, well served by his singers, Michael Kelly and Nancy, who were well versed in methods which they had experienced in *Le nozze di Figaro*.

It would be a decade after Storace's death before audiences would see a Mozart opera on a London stage, and yet he had already paved the way for a radical change in English opera. The tragedy was that there was now no one of his calibre to compose the music.

THOMAS ATTWOOD
Mozart's English Pupil

I N VIENNA, MOZART LIVED IN A MANNER THAT ENABLED HIM TO MOVE WITH ease within the higher ranks of society. He needed their patronage for support of his musical career but, in spite of the fact that his earnings were greater than many of his fellow composers, the extravagance of his lifestyle meant that his financial affairs were sometimes precarious, and for a much needed extra source of income he had, for several years, taken on pupils.[1] At first he charged the sum of six ducats (possibly about £500 in present terms) for twelve lessons, but later, because some pupils defaulted, he changed to a flat fee of six ducats per month. It was with some reluctance that he committed himself to teaching but, as he writes, "I could not get on at all without pupils, which is a kind of work that is quite uncongenial to me". However, he does go on to say, "I will gladly give lessons as a favour, particularly when I see that my pupil has talent, inclination, and anxiety to learn".[2]

In August 1785 such a pupil did arrive in Vienna in the person of a very presentable nineteen-year-old Englishman, Thomas Attwood. It was a particularly busy time for Mozart, and he could well have done without the encumbrance of another student. However, there was the financial necessity, and it is possible that his English friends, the Storaces and Michael Kelly, induced him to take on their fellow countryman. A little later, Leopold Mozart, writing to his daughter Nannerl, quotes a letter from her brother: "he [Mozart] is up to the eyes in work at his opera 'Le nozze di Figaro'. . . . He adds that in order to keep the morning free for composing he is now taking all his pupils in the afternoon".[3]

Thomas Attwood was born in London in November 1765 and, through the auspices of his father, who was a member of His Majesty's Band of Musicians, young Thomas received his early musical education at age nine as a chorister of the Chapel Royal, Windsor. In 1781, when his voice broke, he had to leave the choir and he became Page of the Presence to the Prince of Wales, himself a devotee of music. The following year he took part in a musical performance at Buckingham House. His ability to play the harpsichord so impressed the prince that he was sent, at the royal expense, to

FIG. 11. Thomas Attwood (1765–1838). Unsigned lithograph.
By Permission of the British Library: Department of Manuscripts, Add. MS 35027, f.15r.

study in Italy. He chose to go to Naples, an established centre of opera, where he became friendly with a young Italian musician, Giacomo Ferrari (1763–1842).[4] They took lodgings together and both entered upon a course of instruction with Gaetano Latilla (1711–88), a well-known composer of opera in his day, but he was now in his seventies and no longer writing for the stage, although much respected as a teacher. But after two years in Naples Attwood decided that his future was with Mozart, and he moved to Vienna from where he continued to write to his friend Ferrari. This correspondence throws an interesting light on Attwood's reverence for Mozart and the manner in which some Italians received Mozart's music. In his book of memoirs, *Aneddoti piacevoli e interessante*, Ferrari writes,

I was unfortunate to lose the society of my good friend Attwood, who set out for Vienna in order to complete his studies under the celebrated Mozart. He arrived in the metropolis at the very moment the great composer published his six quartets, dedicated to Haydn, and sent me a copy as a present with a letter in which he advised me not to form an opinion of them until I had heard them executed several times over. I accordingly tried them with some amateur performers as well as professors who were friends of mine, but we could execute only the slow movements and even those indifferently.

Ferrari showed one of the quartets to Latilla who scrutinised it carefully, and then, putting down the copy in astonishment, the old master exclaimed, "This is the most magnificent piece of music I ever saw in my life".[5]

Attwood spent the next nineteen months in Vienna with Mozart, during which time he kept a detailed workbook of his studies. It was with great good fortune that he treasured the manuscript until the end of his life and after passing through the hands of several scholars it is now in the possession of the British Library. There are a total of one hundred and forty-eight folios, forming a complete course in musical composition, which Attwood used subsequently to instruct his own pupils. They constitute a very important document since they provide a unique written record of another aspect of Mozart's life, his ability and methods as a teacher.[6]

A scrutiny of the first folios shows, somewhat surprisingly, that during the two years Attwood was with Latilla he had actually learnt very little from the ageing composer. This is made clear by the fact that Mozart painstakingly started his pupil from scratch, first making him carry out rudimentary exercises in writing out major and minor scales. He then progressed step by step to lessons in harmony with figured bass until he reached the stage of writing free composition with no given bass as a guide, before proceeding to the art of orchestration. All the time Mozart corrected his pupil's many mistakes very assiduously in his fine handwriting, revising much, and writing pertinent comments on the manuscript.

Early in 1786 the time came to subject his pupil to the exacting discipline of counterpoint, the technique by which independent melodic lines are brought together in harmony, classical examples being the canon and the fugue. Mozart himself had received instruction in contrapuntal writing when he was a child from his father and his London vocal work 'God is our Refuge' is an early example of rudimentary polyphony. Later, in 1770, he had lessons from the old master of counterpoint, Padre Martini, in Bologna. These experiences resulted in the writing of his early church music such as the fugue in the Mass in G major, K.49, and the five-part canonic Kyrie, K.89. Within a few years, influenced by Haydn's quartets, he was already utilising counterpoint in his chamber music, such as in the earlier string quartets, K.168 and K.173. But it was not until much later, about 1782, that, stimulated by his friend Baron Gottfried van Swieten, Mozart became really aware of the works of Johann Sebastian Bach. It was then that Bach's tremendous artistry in counterpoint struck him and thereafter his enthusiasm for contrapuntal writing was unabated.[7] Writing to his father about the composition of his Prelude and Fugue in C major, K.394, in April 1782, Mozart says,

My dear Constanze is really the cause of this fugue's coming into the world. The Baron van Swieten, to whom I go every Sunday, gave me all the works of Handel and Sebastian Bach to take home with me (after I had played them to him). When Constanze heard the fugues, she absolutely fell in love with them. . . . I intend to compose five more and then present them to the Baron van Swieten.[8]

His contrapuntal writing was not confined to formal fugues and canons, but is to be found to an increasing extent in his later instrumental compositions, notably in the great string quartets and quintets, reaching the heights in the finale of the 'Jupiter' Symphony; their greatness is a reflection of Mozart's mastery of the techique. Attwood later recalled that Bach's celebrated volume of forty-eight preludes and fugues, *The 48* (BWV 846–93), was always lying open on Mozart's piano.

As far as Attwood was concerned, the learning of counterpoint did not come easily, and his exercises in the technique were initially not very successful, in spite of his time in Naples with Latilla, a supposed master. One of his very imperfect attempts at writing a fugue in an exercise dated 13th August 1786 was immortalised by Mozart when he later reproduced it almost exactly in the final movement of his famous parody of an incompetent composer, *Ein Musikalischer Spass* (*A Musical Joke*), K.522. However, the pupil did eventually prosper, and there are no less than fourteen two-part canons by him in the manuscript as well as beautiful examples of canons written by the master himself, K.507 and K.508.

Personal messages between Mozart and his pupil, written on the pages of the workbook, provide a picture of the close relationship which existed between them. On one occasion Mozart wrote, in English, "This after noon I am not at home, therefore I pray you to come tomorrow at three and a half." Later, Attwood recounts the number of times he visited Mozart's fine apartment in the Schulerstrasse, not just for lessons but to play billiards with his master, who was so addicted to the game that he actually played while composing.[9] Early in his studies, the budding composer wrote on the exercise, somewhat presumptuously, "Thomas Attwood's comp^{ts} to Mr Mozardt, hoping this example will meet his approbation as he has taken all possible Care to leave no room for Correction. Tuesday 23 August in the year of our Lord 1785." This optimism was to prove unfounded many times. On one occasion, during his lessons in counterpoint the manuscript shows that Mozart scored out much of the exercise and, demonstrating his knowledge of colloquial English, wrote twice, emphatically, "You are an ass".

In spite of these forthright criticisms, by the end of 1786 Attwood had progressed well and the workbook shows that there were many fewer corrections to be made. Mozart had, by this time, become very fond of his first English pupil and, according to Michael Kelly, he said,

Attwood is a young man for whom I have a sincere affection and esteem; he conducts himself with great propriety, and I feel much pleasure in telling you that he partakes more of my style than any other scholar I have ever had, and I predict that he will prove a sound musician.[10]

Kelly adds that Mozart was very liberal in giving praise to those who deserved it, but felt a thorough contempt for insolent mediocrity.

In fact, busy as he was at this time with many important compositions, it is clear that, far from being the frivolous irresponsible character that he is sometimes portrayed, Mozart as a teacher is shown to be a most methodical and serious person, at least for someone who was responsive to his efforts. Another valuable contribution which the workbook manuscripts provide is an unrivalled insight into the thinking which guided Mozart in his mature compositions. The many careful revisions that he made and the beautiful examples of contrapuntal writing which he produced show a supreme master at work.

It is also evident that Attwood was on close terms with the Mozart family. In 1821, many years after Mozart's death, his widow Constanze, now remarried, wrote to him,

Mrs Nissen, once Mozart, is truly happy to hear from her old friend Mr Attwood. . . . [H]er elder son which Mr Attwood will recollect to have born in his arms, has left the foot steps of his father, and is employed in his Sovereign's Civil service at Milano. The younger one seeks those foot steps and, as he is not deprived of talents and genius, meets with esteem and applause in a travel he has undertaken through Germany. His mother cannot but desire that their English friend might judge convenient to encourage him to a journey to London. Mrs Nissen begs Mr Attwood to receive her warmest thanks for the constancy of his friendship and her eager wishes for his felicity.[11]

There is no record of any reply and Constanze Mozart's hopes for her younger son's future in England did not materialise.

The time from August 1785 to early 1787 that Attwood spent with Mozart coincided with the most productive period of his master's career. During his course of study Attwood witnessed the inception of *Le nozze di Figaro* and its subsequent first performance, the production of the one-act opera *Der Schauspieldirektor* (*The Impresario*) at the Schönbrunn Palace, and many other important compositions, including the two Piano Quartets (K.478 and K.493), the Horn Concerto No. 4 (K.495), four of the greatest piano concertos (K.482, K.488, K.491 and K.503), the Hoffmeister String Quartet (K.499), a piano sonata for four hands (K.497), and the 'Prague' Symphony (K.504). Attwood provides a little information about Mozart's method of composing. In a letter to an unidentified correspondent, he mentions that, "In consequence of being so much over the table when composing, he was obliged to have an upright desk and stand when he wrote".[12] On another occasion, Attwood remarks upon the speed of Mozart's writing when he says that on entering the composer's apartment one morning he found the floor strewn with sheets of a score, thrown down one by one as they were finished and left to dry. Such works could not have failed to impress the young musician and he remained a devoted admirer of his master for the rest of his life.

In the company of the Storaces and Michael Kelly, in March 1787 Attwood returned to London, where he continued to enjoy the favour of the Prince of Wales, who had now set up his own magnificent establishment at Carlton House. Attwood was appointed to be one of the chamber musicians but, unfortunately, the prince's financial state became so ruinous that his private band had to be abolished and the appointment was soon terminated. Nevertheless, he was able to maintain his position as Page of the Presence, and soon began to publish his own compositions, a series of sonatas and trios for the keyboard. Thereafter, royal patronage ensured that his promotion was steady and in 1791 he was appointed Music Master to the Duchess of York.

On 8th April 1795 the Prince of Wales married his cousin, that extraordinary woman, Caroline of Brunswick, and Attwood was appointed to be her music teacher also. Whatever her faults may have been, and they were many, Princess Caroline, under Attwood's influence, became an ardent follower of Mozart. Fanny Burney, in her *Memoirs of Doctor Burney*, speaks of Charles Burney's summons to a concert at the Princess's establishment at Blackheath where he says,

the music performed was chiefly of Mozart; and her Royal Highness, on piece following piece of the same composer, cried: "I hope you like Mozart Dr Burney?" "No compositions can better deserve your Royal Highness' favour" I answered; for his inventions and resources are inexhaustible; and his vocal music of which we knew nothing in England till he was dead surpasses in beauty even his instrumental, which had so justly, in this country, obtained him the warmest applause.[13]

In 1796 Attwood was appointed composer to the Chapel Royal and Organist to St Paul's Cathedral, positions that he was to occupy for the remainder of his life. In spite of these ecclesiastical posts, he continued to be a very prolific composer for the stage, beginning in 1792 with the opera *The Prisoner*, into which he inserted the splendid aria from *Le nozze di Figaro*, 'No piu andrai', sung to the words 'Where the Banners of Glory are Streaming'. He obviously made use of the manuscript brought back to England by his friends, the Storaces, and it was the first time that music from *Figaro* was published in this country.

Over the space of more than a quarter of a century Attwood produced thirty four works for the stage, most of which were so-called afterpieces, shorter works, often pasticcios, which were performed after the main theatrical production of the evening.[14] Many of the early compositions contained conscious borrowings of music by Mozart. *Caernarvon Casle* (1793) contained the 'Letter' duet from *Figaro*, *The Marriners* (1793) included Sarastro's aria 'In diesen heiligen Hallen' from *Die Zauberflöte*, and the opening chorus of the musical drama *Il Bondocani* (1800) utilised Mozart's Chorus of the Janissaries from *Die Entführung aus dem Serail*. None of the music scores had yet appeared in print in England. In 1800 Attwood's Welsh ballad opera *St David's Day* appeared with a dedication of his grateful thanks to the Prince of Wales: "You introduced my Pupilage to the great, the lamented Mozart, and supported me under his tuition".

A eulogistic review of his contribution to the opera *David Rizzio*, in *The Times* of 19th June 1820, said,

The piece contains airs by Attwood whose character as a composer cannot be more justly or powerfully drawn than by reminding the public of a fact which his own modesty leads him to withold as much as possible—that he is a pupil of Mozart and a pupil worthy of that celebrated master.

But in spite of some favourable comment, Attwood's operatic music was never a real success and it is now virtually forgotten.

It is in the realm of church music that he is mainly remembered, especially for his large-scale anthems, which, true to his teacher, contain much elaborate counterpoint. For the coronation of his patron as George IV in 1821, he wrote the anthem 'I Was Glad', and ten years later, for the coronation of William IV, he wrote another, 'O Lord, Grant the King a Long Life'. He also wrote many short pieces including songs and hymns, such as 'Come, Holy Ghost', in many of which can be discerned the carefully constructed harmony and elegance characteristic of works by Mozart.

Attwood was now a very respected figure in the musical world, and in 1813 he was made a founder member of the Philharmonic Society, (still in existence as the Royal Philharmonic Society), and thereafter conducted many of the Society's concerts. In this capacity he took every opportunity to bring Mozart's music before the English public, conducting all of the last great symphonies. At the inauguration of the Royal Academy of Music in 1823 he was appointed one of the original professors and about this time his old patron, King George IV, made him organist to the private chapel at his favourite residence, the Royal Pavilion, Brighton. In the later years of his life, Attwood became firm friends with the young Mendelssohn, who was himself a great admirer of Mozart. During his first visit to England in 1829, at the age of twenty, Mendelssohn suffered a serious injury following a carriage accident, and he spent time convalescing in Attwood's house at Norwood, South London. It was here that he wrote his Capriccio for Piano and he dedicated his Three Preludes and Fugues for the Organ to his elderly friend.

On 24th March 1838 Attwood died at his new home in Chelsea, while working on a third coronation anthem, for the enthronement of Queen Victoria. He was buried in St Paul's Cathedral under the organ and his own 'Magnificat and Nunc Dimittis' was sung at his funeral. Mendelssohn's affection is shown by the epitaph he wrote: "I know for certain that I should not meet again in this life so kind an artist, so benevolent and amiable a character".[15]

There is no question that Attwood was very fortunate in obtaining an unrivalled musical education and that, as a result, he became a competent composer, but his position in English music as a creative artist is relatively slight. Mozart's assessment of him was exactly right when he predicted that he would be a "sound musician". His most valuable legacy is not his music but the workbook of his youth, which has provided us with yet another facet of the life of his master.

✣ CHAPTER XV ✣
INVITATIONS TO ENGLAND

A T THE END OF FEBRUARY 1787 MOZART PAID SAD FAREWELLS TO HIS much-loved British friends on their departure, and they, in turn, promised that they would soon see him again in London after they had obtained work for him.

Mozart had never lost his affection for England since his long stay in London as a child and for many years he had had a desire to return. In August 1782, soon after he married Constanze, he wrote, "If Germany my beloved fatherland, of which you know I am proud, will not accept me, then in God's name let France or England become richer by another talented German, to the disgrace of the German nation".[1] His enthusiasm for England, in particular, is expressed further when he says, "I have already taken three lessons in English. In three months I hope to be able to read and understand English books fairly easily". He certainly began to practise his written English because in September he ends a letter to his friend and patroness Baroness von Waldstätten with the English sentence, "j kiss your hands, and hoping to see you in good health the Tuesday j am your most humble servant".[2]

Leopold was very concerned about what he regarded as a very ill-considered project on the part of his son to go abroad when, if only he would be patient, a career was open to him in Vienna. At first Mozart appeared to realise the sense of his father's advice: "You are perfectly right about France and England. It is a step which I can always take, and it is better for me to remain in Vienna a little longer".[3]

However, by the 1780s, with the influx of aristocratic Englishmen on the Grand Tour, Vienna had become wildly anglophile, so that it was now very fashionable to imitate English customs, clothes, eating and drinking. As a contemporary, Johann Pezzl, observes in his 'Sketch of Vienna',

The results of this anglomania are to be seen in people reading and speaking English, round hats, large greatcoats of rough material, full neckerchiefs, dark frock-coats, with high collars, boots and spurs at all times. . . . For ladies it means a liking for horse-riding, tea, hats, anglaises [a dance], *speaking English and reading books, and a general preference for any male, young or old, handsome or hideous, who lives anywhere between the Isle of Wight and the Orkneys.*[4]

In this atmosphere, the close association Mozart now had with the English circle turned his mind once more to making a visit to their country. At the end of 1786 reports appeared in the press that "The celebrated composer Herr Mozart is preparing to travel to London in the coming Spring, having the most advantageous offers there. He will go by way of Paris".[5] This report may well have been instigated by Mozart with the purpose of forcing some reaction from the reluctant Emperor Joseph to provide him with a proper appointment in Vienna but the fact that he was serious in his intention to go to England very soon is seen from the next altercation with his father.

Mozart had learnt that Leopold was now taking care of his married sister Nannerl's little son and he decided that a good scheme would be for his own two children also to be looked after by his father while he and Constanze went to London with his English friends. This idea provoked an outburst of indignation from Leopold. Writing to Nannerl on 17th November 1786 he said,

I had to reply today to a letter from your brother, and this took me a considerable time. . . . You can easily imagine that I had to express myself very emphatically, as your brother actually suggested that I should take charge of his two children, because he was proposing to undertake a journey through Germany to England in the middle of next carnival. I wrote therefore very fully and added that I would send him the continuation of my letter by the next post. Herr Muller, that good man and honest maker of silhouettes, had said a lot of nice things about little Leopold [Nannerl's child] *to your brother, who heard in this way that the child is living with me. I had never told your brother. So that is how the brilliant idea occurred to him or perhaps to his wife. Not at all a bad arrangement! They could go off and travel—they might even die—or remain in England—and I should have to run after them with the children. As for the payment which he offers me for the children and for maids to look after them, well— Basta! If he cares to do so, he will find my excuse very clear and instructive.*[6]

So Mozart's immediate plans to make a journey to England came to nought.

It seems, however, that Mozart still had visions of travelling abroad in the near future because two months later, while he was in Prague, he wrote to his friend Baron Gottfried von Jacquin in Vienna,

When I remember that after my return I shall enjoy only for a short while the pleasure of your valued society and then shall have to forgo this happiness for such a long time, perhaps for ever, then indeed I realise the extent of the friendship and regard which I cherish for your whole family.[7]

After Leopold had made the acquaintance of his son's friends in Salzburg on their way home, he writes to his daughter how he had followed up his first letter to Wolfgang:

As for your brother I hear that he is back in Vienna. I had no reply to the letter I sent him to Prague. The English company told me that he made a thousand gulden there, that little Leopold, his last boy, has died, and that, as I had gathered, he wants to travel to England, but that his pupil is first going to procure a definite engagement for him in London, I mean, a contract to compose an opera or a subscription concert, etc. Probably Madame Storace and the whole company had filled him with stories to the same effect and these people and his pupil must have been the first to give him the idea of accompanying them to England. But no doubt after I sent him a fatherly letter, saying that he would gain nothing by a journey in summer, as he would arrive in England at the wrong time, that he ought to have at least two thousand gulden in his pocket before undertaking such an expedition, and finally that, unless he had procured in advance some definite engagement in London, he would have to be prepared, no matter how clever he was, to be hard up at first at any rate, he has probably lost courage, particularly as Madame Storace's brother will of course write the opera for the next season.[8]

For the rest of that year Mozart was taken up with major compositions culminating in his commission for the opera *Don Giovanni*, which had its première in Prague on 29th October. Thereafter his financial position appeared to deteriorate, but it was not until towards the end of 1790 that a definite proposal came from London.

Mozart was away in Frankfurt from September to November on a largely unprofitable mission and on his return a letter was awaiting him. Dated 26th October 1790, it was from the manager of the Italian Opera Company in London, a certain Mr Robert Bray O'Reilly. It was addressed in stilted French to "Monsieur Mozart, Célèbre Compositeur de Musique a Vienne", and read,

Through a person attached to H. R. H. the Prince of Wales I learn of your design to undertake a journey to England, and as I desire to know people of talent personally and am at present in a position to contribute to their advantage, I offer you, Sir, such a position as few Composers have had in England. If you are thus able to be in London towards the end of the month of December next, 1790, and to stay until the end of June 1791, and within that space of time to compose at least two Operas, serious or comic, according to the choice of the Directorate, I offer you three hundred pounds Sterling, with the advantage to write for the professional concerts or any other concert-hall with the exception only of other Theatres. If this proposal seems agreeable to you and you are in a position to accept it, do me the favour of letting me have a reply by return, and this letter shall serve you in place of a Contract. Kindly address your reply to the Pantheon in London.[9]

England was recognised by continental composers to be generous to musicians and the financial offer of three hundred pounds for two operas was about three times the amount Mozart had received for *Le nozze di Figaro* and *Don Giovanni*. However, the reason behind this letter was that at this time the politics of the Italian Opera Company were in ferment. The traditional house, the King's Theatre in the Haymarket, which held the licence to stage Italian opera, had burnt down and was now being feverishly rebuilt. In the meantime a financial consortium, consisting of the Prince of Wales, the Duke of Bedford, and the Marquis of Salisbury were intent on staging Italian opera at the Pantheon, the luxurious concert hall in Oxford Street. Salisbury was the Lord Chamberlain, and therefore had the licensing power, and was intent on transferring it to the Pantheon before the King's Theatre could rise again. Thus, the manager of the Pantheon, Robert O'Reilly, a somewhat inexperienced young Irishman, was under great pressure to recruit top singers and composers as soon as possible.

The identity of the mysterious "person attached to H. R. H. the Prince of Wales" has been the subject of some conjecture. There seems little doubt that Mozart had been corresponding with some or all of his English friends after they had returned to London and the most likely figure would appear to be Thomas Attwood, devotee and pupil of Mozart, who had been sponsored by the prince for his studies in Vienna and who returned to the royal entourage afterwards. Recently, however, the discovery of correspondence from O'Reilly in the Bedford Opera Papers has cast further light on the subject. In his attempts to recruit the services of the best opera singers for his enterprise at the Pantheon, O'Reilly invited Nancy Storace to leave her position at Drury Lane but it seems that one of the terms that she demanded was for her friend Mozart to be the resident composer, and she is known to have been very close to the Prince of Wales.[10]

There is no record whether Mozart replied to O'Reilly but, if he did so, he would not have answered the letter until the second week of November after his return to Vienna, and on the 23rd of that month a notice in a London newspaper announced that Giovanni Paisiello had been appointed as composer. In the event, Paisiello did not take up the appointment.

In October, when he was still away in Frankfurt he wrote to Constanze,

I have often thought of travelling further afield but whenever I tried to bring myself to take the decision the thought always came to me how bitterly I should regret it if I were to separate myself from my beloved wife for such an uncertain prospect, perhaps even to no purpose whatever.[11]

At that time Mozart's wife was in a poor state of health and even if he now had the prospect of a definite contract it is clear that he would not contemplate leaving Constanze in Vienna. If, indeed, he wrote to O'Reilly on his return it is almost certain that he had to decline the invitation.

A further invitation was soon to follow. In December of that year Johann Peter Salomon (1745–1815) came to Vienna to bring Haydn to London. Salomon was a celebrated German violinist and composer who had settled in London and was now a very successful impresario. He had already featured a Mozart symphony in his first subscription concert at the Hanover Square rooms and it was probably he that christened Mozart's last symphony 'Jupiter'. On 14th December there was a farewell dinner given for Haydn on the eve of his departure, at which Mozart was present. Salomon used the occasion to extend a similar invitation to Mozart to come with him to London but, again, it is clear that the answer was negative because on Haydn's departure Mozart said, with tears in his eyes, "We are probably saying our last adieu in this life", presumably referring to what was to him Haydn's advanced age.[12]

Many reasons have been advanced for Mozart's failure to respond to the invitations to London in spite of his often declared interest in returning to England. His earlier intentions had been thwarted by Leopold and it seems that the timing of the specific invitations which came later was wrong for him. Undoubtedly, the state of his wife's health weighed very heavily and he could not bear to be parted from her for long.

During the middle of his last year, 1791, another proposal was put to him. Lorenzo da Ponte who, according to his memoirs, had had serious differences with his employer, the new emperor, Leopold, had recently resigned his post as poet to the Italian Opera Company in Vienna. He thereupon suggested to Mozart that they should resume their highly successful collaboration in London, where they could join their influential friends, the Storaces and Kelly.[13] However, Mozart was then heavily committed to important commissions, including *Die Zauberflöte*, and he still nurtured the hope of obtaining, at long last, a financially worthwhile post in Vienna. He therefore asked da Ponte to defer the idea for six months. By that time, however, Mozart was dead.

It is certain that if Mozart had been able to go to London the demand for foreign composers of his standing was such that he, like Haydn, would have earned a great deal of money. It is even more interesting to consider that if he had stayed in London throughout 1791 he would have escaped the fever epidemic in Vienna which ended his life.[14]

PART FOUR
Epilogue

FIG. 12. Vincent Novello (1781–1861). Unsigned engraving.
By Permission of the British Library: Department of Manuscripts, Add. MS 35027 f.36r.

CHAPTER XVI

VINCENT AND MARY NOVELLO

A T THE END OF THE SECOND WORLD WAR IN THE SMALL ITALIAN TOWN OF
Fermo, near the Adriatic coast, there came to light two remarkable
diaries, those of Vincent and Mary Novello. Vincent Novello (1781–
1861), music scholar and editor, was also organist and choirmaster at the
Portuguese Embassy Chapel in South Street, London, where his playing of
Haydn's and Mozart's masses attracted large audiences. He was also a publisher of music, largely at his own expense, but it was left to his son to put
the business on a commercial basis and establish the well known publishing
firm of Novello.

Novello was a great friend of Mozart's pupil, Thomas Attwood, then
organist at St Paul's, both of them being founder members of the Philharmonic Society, and it was probably through Attwood that he came to know
Mozart's music. Not only did he play Mozart's masses at the Portuguese
Chapel but by publishing them in easily accessible form he brought them
to the notice of a wider public.

In 1808 he married Mary Sabilla Hehl (1789–1854), a strong, determined
woman, who shared all her husband's interests, and between them they attracted some of the greatest musical and literary figures of the time to their
house in London. Mendelssohn visited there during his stay in England, as
did Paganini, Liszt, Shelley and Keats, as well as their close friends Leigh
Hunt and Charles Lamb.

Vincent Novello was a passionate devotee of Mozart, and after twenty
one years of a supremely happy marriage he and Mary decided to make the
pilgrimage to Salzburg, the birthplace of the man they called "the Shakespeare of music".[1] Their immediate objective was to present, in person, a
sum of money donated by like-minded English admirers of Mozart, to his
aged sister Nannerl, the widowed Madame Berchtold zu Sonnenburg who,
they had discovered, was now very ill in Salzburg. A second reason for the
journey was to visit and question that other most valuable link with their
revered composer, Constanze, recently widowed again, but still very much
alive, also in Salzburg. Vincent had recently acquired the biography of
Mozart by G. N. Nissen, Constanze's second husband, and he had plans to

write his own English version. In fact, he never did carry out the task and it was left to his pupil Edward Holmes to produce the first English biography.

It was their journey to Salzburg and then on to Vienna in search of anecdotes from persons who knew Mozart that occupies the greater part of the Novello diaries. Both Vincent and Mary wrote their own independent accounts of most of the interviews so that each provides a check on the other, sometimes with a slightly different emphasis. After they were found in 1945 the diaries were examined by the Novellos' great granddaughter, Nerina Medici di Marignano, and with her help they were edited by Rosemary Hughes to form a fascinating glimpse of Mozart's life, as seen by his living relatives and friends during that year 1829, and recounted by two English devotees.

The Novellos collected a total of sixty guineas to present to the ill, impoverished Nannerl, and it is interesting to see who were the donors. The list of sixteen contributors[2] who were "enthusiastic admirers of the delightful compositions of Mozart" include, besides Novello himself, Attwood, the sole survivor of Mozart's group of English friends in Vienna; John Braham, singer and former lover of Nancy Storace; Johann Baptist Cramer, composer, pianist, and music publisher; Cipriani Potter, pianoforte professor at the Royal Academy of Music; Ignaz Moscheles, composer and pupil of Salieri who had recently settled in London; J. A. Stumpff, friend of Beethoven and collector of Mozart autographs. It was Stumpff who had been in correspondence with Mozart's widow, Constanze, and had learnt of Nannerl's sad plight. They represent an important section of the musical establishment in London at that time.

The Novellos set out for Salzburg on 24th June 1829 and arrived there on 14th July. By this time, the sixty-six-year-old Constanze, who had lost her second husband, Georg Nikolaus Nissen, three years previously, was living in a house in picturesque surroundings under the walls of the Hohensalzburg fortress. Their first meeting with Madame Nissen, as she is called, was to them a very emotional experience,

We have just seen Mozart's widow. . . . the woman that was so dear to him, whom he has so often fondly caressed, for whom his anxiety and tender solicitude urged on to such great and glorious efforts of his genius, next to seeing himself it was the nearest approach to his earthly remains.[3]

Mary Novello characterises Constanze as a completely well-bred lady, speaking French fluently, in which they had to converse, as well as Italian. Vincent describes Constanze's appearance. Her face was thin with traces of great care and anxiety in it, but with very fine eyes, and when her features relaxed into a smile she had a very pleasant expression. She was of rather small stature, slim figure, looking much younger than her age. However, he does add that while she spoke tenderly of her illustrious husband it was "not quite so enthusiastic as I should have expected in one so near and dear to him". Her room was surrounded by Mozart family portraits of which the best likeness of Mozart, in the opinion of his widow, was the one painted towards the end of his life by her brother-in-law, Joseph Lange.[4]

As it happened, Mozart's younger son Franz Xaver Wolfgang (1791–1844) was making one of his infrequent visits to his mother from Lemberg in Poland where he then lived with his mistress, a married Polish countess. The Novellos were delighted to be able to talk with this other member of the Mozart family, but it is clear that they found him a rather pathetic figure. He was only five months old at his father's death, but he seems to have been pushed by his mother into carrying on with his father's profession, even to the extent of using the name Wolfgang Mozart. As Vincent said,

Young Mozart is a melancholy thoughtful-looking person—he is short and rather stout, with very frank, and unaffected, quiet manners, his face somewhat resembling his father's, especially the forehead. He is (unfortunately, I think) a professor of music, and seems to be impressed with the idea, that everything he can possibly do, will be so greatly inferior to what was accomplished by the wonderful genius of his illustrious father, that he feels disinclined to write much, or to publish what he produces.[5]

The next day Mozart's son escorted the Novellos to the home of his aunt, Nannerl. It was a sad occasion because they found her in bed "blind, languid, exhausted, feeble, and nearly speechless". In a very low voice she regretted that they did not speak German but, through her nephew, she was able to express her appreciation of their visit and the present which they had brought from her brother's English admirers. Mary Novello describes her countenance as much changed, even rather ugly, but still somewhat resembling her portrait. She was very fair in appearance with the most delicate hands. Near her bed was the famous picture of her playing the piano with her brother, their father leaning on it, and the portrait of their mother looking down. In the adjoining room was the same piano with its distinguishing feature of black keys for the natural notes and white for the sharps. They learnt that two days before they had arrived Nannerl had insisted on being carried to the keyboard where she had been able to perform a few passages with her right hand, but the power on her left side had completely gone. It is presumed that she had suffered a stroke. Three months later, on 29th October, she died. Back in London, Vincent Novello directed a performance of Mozart's Requiem in her memory at the Portuguese Embassy Chapel.

The Novellos spent three days in Salzburg during which they interviewed Constanze and her son at length with many questions which they had prepared. Young Mozart confirmed that the greatest admirer of his father among the musicians was Haydn, who repeatedly stated that he was the greatest musical genius that ever existed, and that if he (Mozart) had gone to England first, as the impresario Salomon at one time had wished, it would have been no use for him (Haydn) to go there as "nothing would do after Mozart's compositions".

In Constanze's delightful, flower-filled garden on the hillside overlooking the town, she continued to answer their questions. They heard that Mozart's favourite pieces of music were arias from *Don Giovanni*, *Figaro*, and, especially *Idomeneo*, which reminded him of the happy time of his life he spent in Munich; that his favourite instrument was the organ; that he frequently sat up composing until 2 a.m. and rose at 4 a.m. As to his method of composition,

when some grand conception was working in his brain he was purely abstracted, walked about the apartment and knew not what was passing around, but when once arranged in his mind, he needed no pianoforte but would take music paper and whilst he wrote would say to her, "Now, my dear wife, have the goodness to repeat what has been talked of," and her conversation never interrupted him.[6]

Constanze repeated the anecdote in Nissen's biography that Mozart wrote the String Quartet in D minor, K.421, while she was giving birth to their first child and suggested that several passages in the minuet actually portrayed her labour pains.

The well-known tale of the commissioning of the *Requiem* in July 1791 by a messenger from Count Walsegg was again recounted. However, the Novellos were treated to the famous graphic account by Constanze of Mozart's state of mind at the time. She told them that her husband was convinced that he was being poisoned by someone: "I know I muﬅ die, someone has given me acqua toffana and has calculated the precise time of my death—for which they have ordered the Requiem, it is for myself that I am writing this".[7] This ﬅatement to the Novellos has been the source of many of the legends about Mozart's ill-health and death from poisoning. It is impossible to know what was the a&tual basis of Conﬅanze's ﬅory but it takes no account of the fa& that at this time, on 5th July, Mozart himself wrote to Conﬅanze when she was in Baden: "As for my health, I feel pretty well".[8]

Further evidence shows that not all Conﬅanze's reminiscences were accurate. When asked about the composition of the oratorio *Davidde Penitente*, originating from the Mass in C minor, K.427, she said this had been written in fulfilment of a vow after her safe delivery of their firﬅ child, whereas the mass was ﬅarted as a thanks offering on her recovery from illness when she was ﬅill single. Again, when accompanying the Novellos in the nearby Aigen natural park, she maintained that while she and Mozart were living in Salzburg for twelve months (a&tually only three months), her husband, who was a passionate admirer of nature, liked little excursions and passed much of their time out of town. These assertions are not in accordance with anything that Mozart himself wrote.

A slightly curious incident concerns Thomas Attwood, one of the subscribers to the gift for Nannerl, and his relationship with Conﬅanze at this time. As recently as 1821 they had been in correspondence when Conﬅanze had asked Attwood to consider receiving her son, Franz Xaver in London to further his musical career. Nothing came of this, and when the Novellos visited her they showed her a letter of introdu&tion that Attwood had provided them to Aloysia Lange, Conﬅanze's siﬅer, and Mozart's firﬅ love, who was ﬅill living in Vienna. Conﬅanze was obviously disconcerted that Attwood had not written to her and then said it was probable that he did not think she was at Salzburg. It is obvious that Attwood's feelings for her were not as cordial as they had been, since he was fully aware of his friend Vincent Novello's intended visit to Conﬅanze.

After their short ﬅay in Salzburg, the Novellos took leave of Conﬅanze and her son and journeyed to Vienna where they arrived four days later. Here they hoped to carry on their interrogations of people who had been intimately conne&ted with Mozart, but they were to find that some of the Viennese were not particularly well disposed towards Conﬅanze. Their firﬅ call was on their banker, Joseph Henickﬅein, an amateur musician and personal acquaintance of Mozart. He said bluntly that Constanze was no actress and had no great powers as a singer, but he confirmed her description of her husband's pleasant tenor voice and lively character. He also said Mozart played the violin very well and the viola even better.

They next were introduced to Joseph Eybler, Mozart's pupil, who was the first person Constanze approached after Mozart's death to finish the *Requiem*, but who declined the task, subsequently to be taken up by Süssmayr. Much to their delight, he showed them his prize possession, the autograph copy of part of the *Requiem*, starting at the Lacrymosa and ending with 'fac eas', the last note that Mozart ever wrote. He did not explain to them how he came to retain the manuscript.

One morning, while Vincent was out in Vienna searching for the house where Mozart died, Mary received a visit from another link with the past, Aloysia Lange. Then aged sixty nine, she is described by Mary Novello as "a very pleasant woman but broken by misfortune—she is parted from her husband who allows her so little that she is obliged to give lessons which at her age she finds a great hardship".[9] Aloysia Lange reminisced nostalgically about her relationship with Mozart,

she told me Mozart always loved her until the day of his death, which to speak quite candidly she fears has occasioned a slight jealousy on the part of her sister. I asked her why she refused him, she could not tell, the fathers were both agreed but she could not love him at that time, she was not capable of appreciating his talent and his amiable character, but afterwards she much regretted it. She spoke of him with great tenderness and regret.[10]

Time had obviously misted her memory. The fathers were certainly not agreed on the match—Leopold Mozart, in particular, was horrified at the prospect—and after his marriage to Constanze there is no evidence that Mozart had any feelings for Aloysia Lange other than towards a talented singer for whom he wrote music. In fact on one occasion he accused her of being "a false, malicious woman, and a coquette".[11]

At a dinner party the Novellos were introduced to Abbé Maximilian Stadler (1748–1833), an aged theologian and musician who had advised Constanze on the publication of her husband's manuscripts after his death. He had first met Mozart in 1767 when, at age eleven, the boy had played the organ at the great abbey of Melk, and where the abbé subsequently served as prior. Abbé Stadler told how on one occasion when he was present with Mozart and Johann Albrechtsberger, the eminent organist and master of counterpoint, the latter, without warning, gave Mozart a trivial theme he had invented on the spot. Whereupon,

this extraordinary genius immediately took the theme that had been given him thus unexpectedly, and played for upwards of an hour upon it, treating it in all possible variety of form — fugue, canon, from the most simple to the most elaborate counterpoint.

The abbé was also well acquainted with Beethoven, whom he considered to be an extraordinary genius, but irregular and extravagant. He contrasted his method of working with that of Mozart:

Beethoven often began before he knew his own mind and altered backwards and forwards the passages placing them in different places as mere fancy or whim directed—but Mozart never began to write anything till he had arranged the whole design in his mind just as he wished it and then let it stand without alteration.

Other acquaintances of both Mozart and Beethoven to whom the Novellos were introduced were the pianist and teacher, Andreas Streicher, and his wife Maria Anna (Nanette), neé Stein. She was a close confidant of Beethoven until he died, and she had met Mozart in Augsburg when he heard her play the piano at the age of eight. Here she was regarded as something of a child prodigy, but Mozart was very scathing about her technique of playing and the manner in which she had been taught:

She may succeed, for she has great talent for music. But she will never progress by this method. . . . [S]he will never acquire the most essential, the most difficult and the chief requisite in music, which is, time, because from her earliest years she has done her utmost not to play in time.[13]

Perhaps Mozart's strictures bore fruit because Vincent Novello says that Haydn later much admired her piano playing, and he himself attested to her excellent performance when he heard her play. She had inherited her father's famous piano-making firm—the Stein piano had been a favourite instrument of Mozart—and was subsequently joined in the business by her husband.

Andreas Streicher had taught Mozart's son, Franz Xaver, and was well acquainted with Conſtanze, but his opinions of Mozart's widow were much less favourable than the Novellos would have wished. Vincent says little except that the subjeƈt seemed to be a sore one. Mary adds, "Mr Streicher says it was Madame's fault that no monument is ereƈted to Mozart." The Novellos were obviously very unwilling to hear anything ill spoken of Conſtanze, but even they muſt have been aware of the incongruity between the memorial to her two husbands. Vincent had experienced a completely fruitless visit to St Mark's cemetery, finding no trace or record of Mozart's burial, whereas in Salzburg they had been conduƈted by Conſtanze to the impressive pyramidal monument, suitably inscribed, to Georg Nissen. Moreover, much to Nannerl's displeasure, the burial had taken place in the Mozart family vault.

On 30th July the Novellos left Vienna. On their return journey by way of the abbey of Melk they inspeƈted the handsome organ which Mozart had once played. They arrived back in Salzburg four days later and set off immediately for a laſt visit to Mozart's widow. On arriving at her house, they found that she was out miniſtering to her siſter-in-law, Nannerl, but her younger siſter Sophie Haibel was there to greet them. In the course of conversation she mentioned that Mozart was similar in build to his younger son but even shorter.

It was Sophie Haibel who, four years previously, had sent a letter to Georg Nissen giving details of the moments leading up to Mozart's death, to be incorporated into his biography. Whether or not Vincent Novello had read her contribution in the copy of the biography he had acquired, she repeated the well rehearsed ſtory but emphasised that Mozart had died in *her* arms.

Conſtanze returned and when looking through some of the manuscripts in her possession she came upon a copy of the aria 'Al desio' written by Mozart as a subſtitute aria in *Le nozze di Figaro*. It was the aƈtual copy from which he accompanied his wife when she used to sing it to him. It contained a little cadenza at the end in his own handwriting written at her requeſt. Much to Vincent's pleasure, Conſtanze presented him with the manuscript, together with an aria written by Mozart's son for a home performance of his father's short opera *Der Schauspieldirektor*.

More treasure was to follow when Vincent again visited the house of Mozart's siſter, Nannerl. He was not able to see her because she was asleep, but a friend who was in attendance presented him on Nannerl's behalf with a portrait of her brother which had been in her own possession for many years. This was an engraving after the plaster medallion made by Leonard Posch.

The Novellos invited Constanze and her sister Sophie to dinner. Vincent then escorted them back to their house, and says that a beautiful moon was shining on the distant mountains, illuminating the fortress above. They were now so firmly rooted in Constanze's affections that she was able to confide in Vincent her worries about her son and his Polish mistress who seemed to be blighting his future. To Vincent it was a perfect end to their encounters with the Mozart family.

They returned to London, fired with even greater enthusiasm for Mozart's works and intent on disseminating further his music in England. In 1843 Vincent Novello presented the manuscripts he had been given by Mozart's widow to the British Museum and they now form part of the substantial Mozart collection in the British Library.

In attempting to assess the importance of the Novellos' diaries, it should be remembered that they were not only wildly enthusiastic about their hero but that they also shared the early-nineteenth century Romantic notion of famous composers. Their interviews were conducted on a fairly superficial level with little attempt to probe very deeply into the characters of their subjects. Certainly, some of what Constanze Mozart told them was what they wanted to hear and its accuracy is questionable. For example, even such a personal matter as the nature of her husband's hands, which Constanze affirmed were very delicate, as the Novellos supposed, is not born out by a medical observer, Dr Joseph Frank, a pupil of Mozart, who states categorically that his hands were "fleshy".[14] Many of the anecdotes were in any case to be found in Nissen's biography; although Vincent Novello had recently purchased a copy, it was written in German, a language with which he was not very familiar. There are undoubtedly some additions to knowledge about Mozart's life which his English admirers were able to unearth, but perhaps the most interesting aspect of the diaries is the vivid account which they give of the appearance and lives of the many characters who still survived in that year 1829 to tell the Mozart story.

❧ CHAPTER XVII ❧

MOZART'S MUSIC IN ENGLAND
AFTER HIS DEATH

O N 24TH DECEMBER 1791, THE LONDON *TIMES* CARRIED THE ANNOUNCE-
ment: "Died. On the 5 inst at Vienna, Wolfgang Mozart, the celebrated German composer". More fulsome was the notice in the
Morning Post and Daily Advertiser of the same date:

*We have just lost the celebrated Mozart who died suddenly at the age of 36.
This famous Musician, who was considered the greatest genius as a Composer
that we ever possessed, had finished a few weeks before his death, four pieces in
which he even surpassed himself in modulation and force of expression. He is
as much regretted by the Court as by the public.*

It was unheard of at the time for the death of a foreign composer abroad
to feature in the London newspapers, and these notices are an indication of
the high reputation that Mozart already held in England. A very false impression is obtained from Charles Burney's statement in Abraham Rees'
Cyclopaedia, published in 1819:

*In England we knew nothing of his studies or productions, but from his harpsi-
hord lessons, which frequently came over from Vienna; and in these he seems to
have been trying experiments. They were full of new passages and new effects;
but were wild, capricious, and not always pleasing. We were wholly unaquainted
with his vocal music till after his decease.*[1]

In fact, Mozart's mature instrumental music had been performed in
London as early as 16th February 1784, when a symphony was played at
one of the Hanover Square Grand Concerts, sponsored by Lord Abing-
don, successors to the Bach-Abel concerts. Further performances of
Mozart symphonies took place on three subsequent months of that year,
and a review of the concert on 28th April in *The Public Advertiser* stated
that "Mozart's Overture pleased us by many brilliant Passages, not wan-
dering from the Line of either Taste or Judgment". Thereafter, frequent
references appear in the newspapers to newly arrived published works by

Mozart including the piano concertos K.413, K.414, K.415 and the piano sonatas K.309, K.310, K.311, as well as favourable reviews of their performances.[2]

It is clear that interest in Mozart's music was growing steadily. In summer of 1785 John Pettinger (1759–1831), an agent of several London music publishers, visited the composer in Vienna. His first hand impression of Mozart is of interest:

It was a hot day but Mozart was quite formally dressed. He had been hard at work on some compositions for string quartet but seemed not at all put out at being interrupted.Indeed he continued to put down occasional notes during our conversation. I was surprised, when he rose to find him of not more than about five feet and four inches in height and of very slight build. His hand was cold but his grip was firm. His face was not particularly striking, rather melancholy until he spoke, when his expression became animated and amused and his eyes, which constantly darted from Klein [Pettinger's companion] to myself, were full of kind concern in our doings about which he enquired with obvious interest. He had not been to London since a boy but seemed to remember it well and spoke of his old friend Bach, who had died some three years past, and was greatly interested in my dealings with him. I think he would have chatted of this and that for many hours but as we had later appointments that day, Klein turned our talk to the business in hand.[3]

In 1786 Johann Peter Salomon took over the Hanover Square concerts. Under his direction, the orchestra continued to perform Mozart symphonies and on 13th February the Piano Concerto in A major, newly published in England (K.414), was played by Johann Baptist Cramer (1771–1858). *The Morning Post and Daily Advertiser* observed, "The charming Concerto by Mozart, as performed last night at the Hanover Square Concert, was no less admired as a fine composition, than for the exquisite performance of young Cramer".[4] By February 1788 further publications of Mozart's works were available in London which included two symphonies, K.319 and K.385 (the 'Haffner'), the six 'Haydn' quartets, the Piano Quartet, K.478, and the Piano Duet K.501. It was in December 1790 that Salomon, realising the appeal of Mozart for his concert audiences extended an invitation to the composer to join Haydn in London.

We have already seen that after their return from Vienna, early in 1787, Mozart's English friends, the Storaces, Attwood and Kelly, set about promoting his works. Stephen Storace published some of the clavier compositions and his sister Nancy sang arias from *Don Giovanni* and *Le nozze di Figaro* in pasticcio operas.

But the enthusiasm for Mozart in England during his lifetime was nothing compared with that seen in the three decades after the composer's death. Such was the demand that by 1830 there were no less than twenty three publishers of Mozart's music in London. A limited number of his instrumental works continued to be circulated and, in 1801, perhaps because of the popular appeal of oratorio, the *Requiem* was performed for the first time in England. As far as church music was concerned, Vincent Novello published eighteen of the Masses in the form of inexpensive vocal scores even though eight, including the very popular 'Twelfth Mass', were not authentic.

However, it was the belated recognition of his operas which greatly fired the public enthusiasm for Mozart in the early part of the nineteenth century. The first of his operas to be staged at the King's Theatre in London was *La clemenza di Tito*, on the 27th March 1806, at the instigation of the Prince of Wales. His mistress, the well-known soprano Mrs Elizabeth Billington, sang the prima donna role of Vitellia, accompanied by the tenor John Braham as Sesto. In the early nineteenth century, opera seria could still command the attention of London audiences, as this newspaper review of the performance indicates:

The Benefit of Billington, the Goddess of Song, was last night as numerously attended as on most former occasions, proving at once her great popularity. The attraction was the Grand Serious Opera of 'La clemenza di Tito,' composed by Mozart. Braham was loudly encored in one of his songs in the First Act; and Billington was as warmly applauded as ever. All the People of Fashion in Town were present.[5]

La clemenza di Tito was followed on 9th May 1811 by *Così fan tutte*, also at the King's Theatre. *Die Zauberflöte* was premiered on 6th June; the fashion for Italian opera at the time is exemplified by the fact that this last opera was staged as *Il flauto magico*, although it was not initially popular with London audiences. *Le nozze di Figaro* appeared for the first time on 18th June 1812. *Don Giovanni* was the last of the great operas to be produced, not appearing until 12th April 1817, in spite of the fact that da Ponte himself had unsuccessfully tried to stage *Don Giovanni* in London as early as 1794. It surpassed all the others in favour, being repeated twenty-three times in that first season. By 1820 the five operas had reached the pinnacle of their popularity. However, the versions which were given were often very different from our knowledge of the works. The librettos were sometimes rewritten, the orchestration "improved" and even extra music was added. In 1821 *Così fan tutte* was "altered and adapted" and performed at Covent Garden as *Tit for Tat, or The Tables Turned*, to greater acclaim than the original production. *Die Entführung aus dem Serail (The Seraglio)* was first performed on 24th November 1827 at Covent Garden, but in a form so changed in music and words that it was hardly recognisable and the authentic version was not heard until 1887.[6] *Idomeneo* remained in oblivion, and although arias from the opera were frequently given at concerts, the complete work was not produced, perhaps because of the difficulty in its staging. In fact, *Idomeneo* is a relatively recent addition to the Mozart repetoire in England, the first production in a commercial theatre not being given until 1951 at Glyndebourne.

During the first three decades of the nineteenth century, the circle of musicians and literary figures which centred round Vincent and Mary Novello played a large part in disseminating Mozart's music. In 1813 Novello and his friend Thomas Attwood were founder members of the Philharmonic Society, which lost no time in promoting Mozart's orchestral works in its concerts. The first of these on 8th March 1813 contained a string quartet, a serenade for wind instruments, and an aria from *Idomeneo*.[7] Thereafter for the next twenty years, a Philharmonic Society concert usually contained two or three Mozart works, including the last great symphonies, chamber music and, most of all, arias from the operas. At the concert of 13th May 1833, Mendelssohn conducted his own newly commissioned Symphony in A, the 'Italian', and this was preceded by Mendelssohn himself playing Mozart's Piano Concerto in D minor (K.466). A particular devotee of Mozart, Johann Baptist Cramer, continued to be influential in the introduction of Mozart's piano concertos to London audiences, by publishing six of them in 1825 and performing them at Philharmonic Society concerts.[8] Another fine pianist and composer in the Philharmonic Society was Cipriani Potter (1792–1871), a pupil of Attwood, and later teacher of the piano at the Royal Academy of Music, who visited Beethoven several times in Vienna, and who also helped to popularize the Mozart piano concertos through the Society concerts.

Eminent literary members of the Novello circle were no less forthcoming in their praise of Mozart. Leigh Hunt (1784–1859), poet, critic and editor of the *Examiner*, a publication which brought the works of Keats and Shelley to the notice of the public, wrote music criticism for his journal in which he showed his devotion to Mozart. Of *The Magic Flute* he said,

it anticipates for us something of the good, which the human mind, as long as it is worth anything, is so anxious to realise, something of a brighter and more innocent world, in which the good-natured and flowery will is gratified. . . . It is to Mozart's other works what 'The Tempest' is to the most popular of Shakespeare's comedies.[9]

Leigh Hunt's protege, Shelley, often proclaimed his love for Mozart's works, especially *Figaro*, and his fellow poet John Keats similarly expressed his feelings. In his poem, 'Epistle to Charles Cowden Clarke', his boyhood friend and Novello's son-in-law, Keats writes, "But many days have passed since last my heart / Was warm'd luxuriously by divine Mozart". Again, in a letter to his brother George, dated 18th October 1818, Keats reveals his thoughts about a young girl, Jane Cox, "She kept me awake one night as a tune of Mozart's might do".[10]

In their several ways, the Novello circle greatly increased the awareness of Mozart as a great musical figure. In 1845 Edward Holmes (1799–1859), a pupil of Novello and an accomplished music critic, published the first biography of Mozart in English. It was sufficiently well received to demand further editions up to 1912.[11]

The rising cult of Mozart in England was apparent not only in publications and performances of his works; his influence was also felt on the composition of British music during the first part of the nineteenth century.[12] We have already seen how Stephen Storace and Thomas Attwood used their first-hand knowledge of Mozart to incorporate his ideas into their own musical compositions in the late eighteenth century. During the period up to 1840 English composers of the next generation also took Mozart as their model, particularly for instrumental and church music. The keyboard compositions of Johann Baptist Cramer, which include one hundred and twenty four sonatas and nine piano concertos, closely follow Mozart's style. For example, the finale theme of his Piano Sonata, Op. 1, No. 1, strongly echoes Mozart's Sonata in A minor, K.310, and several of the passages in his concertos are taken from the Piano Concerto in D minor, K.466. The piano works of the Irish composer John Field (1782–1837) who later emigrated to St Petersburg, where his nocturnes became greatly admired, show definite Mozartean characteristics, particularly in the use of the minor key and the way in which technical devices such as the tonic pedal were used. One of the most gifted composers of the time was Samuel Wesley (1766–1837), a nephew of John Wesley, the founder of Methodism. His highly regarded Symphony in B flat (1808), in four movements, also displays Mozart's symphonic style and use of the tonic pedal.

The most interesting of the early nineteenth century composers who showed affinities with Mozart was that short-lived musical prodigy George Frederick Pinto (1785–1806).[13] As a child, Pinto was brought up partly by his step-grandmother, the celebrated singer Charlotte Brent, and aged eight became a pupil of Johann Salomon. His surviving compositions, which were all written in just over three years, comprise sixteen charming songs, nine violin duets, four sonatas for piano and violin and works for solo keyboard including six sonatas for solo piano. Three of these sonatas especially, the two of Op. 3 in E flat minor and A major, and the Sonata in C minor, dedicated to his friend John Field, are of astonishing virtuosity and originality, which show unmistakeably Mozartean characteristics. Pinto's early death, like that of the young Linley and Stephen Storace, was a severe blow to English music.

Somewhat later came Frederick Ouseley (1825–89), Thomas Attwood Walmisley (1814–56), godson and pupil of Thomas Attwood, and Samuel Sebastian Wesley (1810–76), all of whom turned particularly to church music very much founded on Mozart.

The most distinguished of the English composers at this time was William Sterndale Bennett (1816–75), who, at an early age unashamedly proclaimed his affinity to Mozart.[14] It is seen most closely in his string quartet, written at the age of fifteen, as well as his first two symphonies. His debut at the Philharmonic Society concert in 1835 was a performance of his own piano concerto. But by now he had come under the influence of Mendelssohn and his later works show only traces of Mozart. He went on to become principal conductor of the Philharmonic Society and was knighted in 1871.

By 1870 the direct influence of Mozart on English composers had largely gone. The public appetite for Beethoven, Mendelssohn, Chopin and, later, Brahms, caused a steady decline in the enthusiasm for Mozart's instrumental music. Likewise, as the century proceeded the operas lost their appeal in favour of those by Rossini and the new works of Wagner and Verdi.

The year 1891 was the centenary of Mozart's death, but by now appreciation of his music had sunk to a low ebb. On this occasion George Bernard Shaw, in many ways a very perceptive music critic, wrote in the *Illustrated London News*,

At present his music is hardly known in England except to those who study it in private. Public performances are few and far between . . . the incompetence and superficiality of Mozart's interpreters are the true and only causes of the apparent triviality of his greatest music. Properly executed, Mozart's work never disappointed anybody yet. Its popularity is increasing after a long interval.[15]

On another occasion Shaw referred to *Don Giovanni* as "the greatest opera in the world". The Philharmonic Society, which had performed but one work by Mozart, a single aria, during that whole year, made amends by devoting the entire first concert of 1892 to him.[16]

With the coming of the new century, the importance of Mozart to opera and concert audiences gradually began to be reasserted. A young, dynamic conductor, Thomas Beecham (1879–1961), embarked on his lifelong efforts to bring Mozart's music to the fore, setting new standards in orchestral playing and interpretation. His memorable season at His Majesty's Theatre in 1910 brought highly praised productions of *The Seraglio*, *Le nozze di Figaro*, and, above all, the opera particularly loved by Beecham, *Così fan tutte*, which had not been seen in London for many years. Knighted in 1916, Sir Thomas continued throughout his long life to conduct Mozart's works, instrumental and operatic, at every opportunity. He asserted that about eleven of the piano concertos were "the most beautiful compositions of their kind in the world". Even today Beecham's recordings of Mozart's music continue to be highly regarded. In 1959, on the occasion of his eightieth birthday, Sir Thomas was given a lavish party at which scores of telegrams were read out from well-wishers from all over the world, at the end of which Beecham observed, "What? Nothing from Mozart?"[17]

In 1934 the Glyndebourne festival was founded by John Christie. It was initially devoted entirely to Mozart and set impeccable standards of production, quality of singing and choice of operas, admittedly for the fortunate few. The beauty of *Così fan tutte* in its original form was reaffirmed, and in 1951 Glyndebourne produced the first professional performance in England of *Idomeneo*, to great acclaim.

In the years between the wars, Mozart's reputation steadily grew as his music was performed before large audiences in locations such as the London Promenade Concerts, but above all it was radio and the gramophone which brought Mozart's music to the masses. Even so, there was a tendency to stay with the main five operas, and in spite of the efforts of people like Beecham, there was little general inclination to explore the instrumental works beyond the last few symphonies, five or six of the piano concertos, and a restricted range of chamber music.

The bicentenary of Mozart's birth in 1956 provided a further impetus to the rise in his appreciation in Britain. Gradually performers and audiences became more adventurous but, in more recent times, the event which was to cause major reverberations in the appreciation of Mozart in Britain, and indeed throughout the musical world, was not a musical performance but a stage play, *Amadeus*. This work, by the playwright Peter Shaffer, opened in London in 1979. It gave a sensational, very inaccurate portrayal of Mozart's life, its central theme being a largely fictitious account of his relationship with Salieri, but it did reach audiences that had never previously encountered Mozart. The film of the play followed within a year or two and, even more extravagantly, it promoted Mozart as a kind of wayward, loutish pop star, but it brought his ravishing music to an international audience of film goers of all ages, many of whom had scarcely known the existence of Mozart. The result was a form of popular Mozartomania, to the virtual exclusion of thought about any other composer.

Just as it seemed that the universal enthusiasm for Mozart was at last subsiding, 1991, the bicentenary of Mozart's death, arrived. Fuelled by the recent experience of the public's exposure to Mozart on a grand scale, the year saw an unprecedented assault by media of various kinds. Books on every aspect of Mozart's life continued to appear, there were festivals throughout the land and recordings of his music. Phillips issued recordings of "every note that Mozart ever wrote". These activites took place not only in Britain but throughout the world. While some was of a trivial nature, and can be dismissed, there is no doubt that some good came of the intense spotlight which was brought to the composer's life and music. The effects of Shaffer's *Amadeus* had largely been to popularise the already well known, but now attention was also given to little performed works, sometimes to great effect. Covent Garden celebrated the occasion by giving the first fully staged professional performance in Britain of the early opera, *Mitridate, rè di Ponto*, in a lavish production which was widely applauded.

More recently, as a result of the interest generated in the early operas, there has been the first British production on the commercial stage of *La finta giardiniera*. An opera until then almost totally neglected in this country, *La finta giardiniera* is a work that is so delightful that an eminent critic at that performance maintained that it should take its place in the regular Mozart repertoire, even taking precedence over *The Seraglio*.

In addition to the search for lesser known compositions, the modern trend has been to provide more and more controversial productions of familiar operas. Fortunately, there has been no reversion to the pernicious tampering with the music and libretto of former times, but the setting of *Così fan tutte* on a modern liner or *Die Zauberflöte* in California has not been received well by the more traditionally minded opera-goers.

Today, Britain, with its long association with Mozart and his own particular affinity for this country, can be proud that once more his works take pride of place in the affections of its music-loving citizens.

NOTES AND BIBLIOGRAPHY

NOTES

CHAPTER I *The Journey to London*

1. *Letters*, p. 51.
2. Ibid., p. 20.
3. Deutsch, p. 550.
4. *Briefe*, vol. 1, p. 104.
5. Deutsch, p. 26.
6. *Letters*, p. 34.
7. Ibid., p. 44.
8. Ibid., p. 37.
9. *Briefe*, vol. 1, p. 145.
10. *Letters*, p. 44.
11. Tobias Smollett, *Travels through France and Italy* (1776), (Oxford, 1981), p. 4.
12. *Letters*, p. 45.
13. Smollett, *Travels*, p. 3.

CHAPTER II *The Musical Scene in London 1764–65.*

1. Roger Fiske, *English Theatre Music in the Eighteenth Century*, 2nd ed. (Oxford, 1986), pp. 150–54.
2. Burney, vol. 2, p. 867.
3. Horace Walpole, *Correspondence*, letter to Earl of Hertford, 27 January 1765. ed. W. S. Lewis, 48 vols. (London and Oxford, 1937–83).
4. Burney, vol. 2, p. 867.
5. Ibid., 2, p. 869.
6. Simon McVeigh, 'Felice Giardini: A Violinist in Late Eighteenth-Century London', *Music and Letters*, 64 (1983), p. 162.
7. Burney, vol. 2, p. 849.
8. Portrait of Giardini in possession of Lord Sackville.
9. Mary Woodall, ed. *The Letters of Thomas Gainsborough*, rev. ed. (1963), p. 165.
10. Burney, vol. 2, p. 868.
11. Ibid., p. 1016.
12. *Briefe*, vol. 1, p. 194.
13. C. F. Pohl, *Mozart and Haydn in England* (Vienna, 1867), vol. 1, p. 38.
14. Tobias Smollett, *Humphrey Clinker*, 1771, (Oxford, 1984). Letter 31 May, p. 92.
15. Portrait of Tenducci in possession of Barbour Institute of Fine Arts, University of Birmingham.
16. *Letters*, p. 54.

17. Burney, vol. 2, p. 867.

18. Ibid., vol. 2, p. 868.

19. Walpole, *Correspondence*, letter to Earl of Hertford, 25 November 1764.

20. Simon McVeigh, *Concert Life in London from Mozart to Haydn* (Cambridge, 1993).

21. P. H. Highfill, K. A. Burnim, and E. A. Langhans, *A Biographical Dictionary of Actors, Actresses, Musicians Dancers, Managers, and other Stage Personnel in London, 1660–1800*, (Carbondale, Ill., 1973–93), vol. 3, pp. 502–08.

22. Burney, vol. 2, p. 844.

23. Fanny Burney, *Early Journals and Letters*, ed. L. E. Troide, 3 vols. (Oxford, 1988–93), vol. 2, p. 120.

24. R. Elkin, *The Old Concert Halls of London* (London, 1955), p. 44.

25. Earl of Malmesbury, *A Series of Letters of 1st Earl of Malmesbury, Family and Friends from 1745 to 1820*, vol. 1, p. 107.

26. Fanny Burney, *Early Journals and Letters*, vol. 3, p. 7.

27. *Letters*, p. 52.

28. James Boswell, *London Journal, 1762–63*, ed. F. A. Poole (London, 1950), p. 279.

29. Fanny Burney, *Evelina* (1778) 2 vols. (Oxford, 1968), vol. 2, p. 231.

30. Samuel Pepys, *Diary*, ed. R. Latham and W. Matthews, 11 vols. (London, 1970–83), vol. 6, p. 132.

31. James Boswell, *Life of Johnson*, ed. G. B. Hill, 6 vols. (Oxford, 1934), vol. 3, p. 231.

32. Smollett, *Humphrey Clinker*, p. 93.

33. Boswell, *London Journal*, p. 279.

CHAPTER III *Performances in London*

1. *Letters*, p. 46.

2. Ibid., p. 47.

3. *Public Advertiser*, 9 May 1764.

4. *Letters*, p. 47.

5. *Public Advertiser*, 31 May 1764.

6. *Letters*, p. 48.

7. *Public Advertiser*, 26 June 1764.

8. *Letters*, p. 49.

9. Ibid., p. 51.

10. Ibid., p. 50.

11. Deutsch, p. 37.

12. *Public Advertiser*, 15 February 1765.

13. *Letters*, pp. 55–56.

14. *Public Advertiser*, 20 March 1765.

15. Deutsch, p. 48.
16. *Public Advertiser*, 8 July 1765.
17. Daines Barrington, 'An account of a remarkable young man', *Philosophical Transactions of the Royal Society*, LX (1771), pp. 54–64.

CHAPTER IV The Compositions in London

1. Deutsch, pp. 38–39.
2. Arranged and recorded by Erik Smith.
3. Deutsch, p. 494.
4. *Public Advertiser*, 13 May 1765.
5. N. Zaslaw and W. Cowdery, eds., *The Compleat Mozart* (New York, 1990), p. 299.
6. G. Nottebohm, *Mozartiana* (Leipzig, 1880), p. 139.

CHAPTER V The Influence of J. C. Bach

1. *Letters*, 48–49.
2. Ibid., p. 47.
3. E. Warburton, 'J. C. Bach's Operas', *Proceedings of the Royal Musical Association*, 92 (1965–6), pp. 95–106.
4. Deutsch, p. 57.
5. W. Jackson, *The Leisure Hour* (London, 1882), p. 274.
6. S. Roe, 'J. C. Bach, 1735–82: Towards a New Biography', *Musical Times*, 123 (1982), pp. 23–26.
7. *Letters*, p. 497.
8. C. S. Terry, *John Christian Bach*, rev. H. C. Robbins, 2nd ed. (London, 1967), p. 80.
9. *Letters*, p. 606.
10. Charlotte L. H. Papendiek, *Court and Private Life in the Time of Queen Charlotte: Being the Journals of Mrs Papendiek*, ed. V. D. Broughton, 2 vols. Vol. 1, p. 150.
11. Ibid., vol. 1, p. 152.
12. *Letters*, p. 800.

CHAPTER VI The Mozart Family Life in London

1. *Briefe*, vol. 1, pp. 145–91.
2. Ibid., p. 173.
3. Ibid., p. 159.
4. Ibid., p. 158.
5. Ibid., p. 183.
6. Ibid., p. 198.
7. Ibid., p. 186.

8. Ibid., p. 179.
9. J. S. Jenkins, 'Leopold Mozart: a Patient in Eighteenth-Century London', *Journal of Medical Biography*, 5 (1997), pp. 30–32.
10. Admitted to Register of Company of Surgeons 1757, Library of Royal College of Surgeons, London.
11. Noted in ratebooks for City of Westminster, 1763–70, Westminster City Library.
12. *Briefe*, vol. 1, pp. 192–96.
13. O. E. Deutsch, *Mozart und seine Welt in zeitgenossischen Bildern* (Kassel, 1961), plate 611.
14. Boswell, *Life of Johnson*, vol. 3, p. 141.
15. *Briefe*, vol. 1, p. 190.
16. I. Woodfield, 'New Light on the Mozart's London Visit', *Music and Letters*, 76 (1995), pp. 187–208.
17. Walpole, *Correspondence*, letter to George Montagu 24 September 1761.
18. Ibid., letter to Sir Horace Mann, 3 May 1749.
19. *Letters*, p. 124.
20. A. Hyatt King, *A Mozart Legacy* (London, 1984), pp. 20–23.
21. Deutsch, p. 46.
22. C. Roscoe, 'Two Eighteenth-Century Non–events', *Musical Times*, 112 (1971), pp. 18–19.

CHAPTER VII *Florence*

1. Elizabeth Gibson, 'Earl Cowper in Florence and His Correspondence with the Italian Opera in London', *Music and Letters*, 68 (1987), pp. 235–52.
2. *Boddely's Bath Journal*, 25 July 1763.
3. Gwilym Beechey, 'Thomas Linley, Junior, 1756–1778', *Musical Quarterly*, 54 (1968), pp. 74–82.
4. Clementina Black, *The Linleys of Bath* (London, 1971).
5. Vernon Lee, *Studies of the Eighteenth Century in Italy* (1907), pp. 90–91.
6. Charles Burney, *Musical Tours in Europe*, ed. P. A. Scholes, 2nd vol. (Oxford, 1959), vol. 1, p. 187.
7. *Letters*, pp. 129–30.
8. Deutsch, p. 115.
9. *Letters*, p. 160.
10. Burney, *Musical Tours*, vol. 1, p. 184.
11. Gwilym Beechey, 'Thomas Linley, 1756–1778, and his Vocal Music', *Musical Times* 119 (1978), pp. 669–71.
12. A. Einstein, Mozart: *His Character, His Work* (London, 1946), p. 136.
13. Michael Kelly, *Reminiscences*, ed. Roger Fiske (Oxford, 1975), p. 112.

CHAPTER VIII *Rome*

1. Burney, *Musical Tours*, vol. 1, p. 232.
2. Charles de Brosses, *Lettres Familières*, eds. G. Cafosso and L. N. Cagiano de Azevede (Naples, 1991), pp. 725–6.
3. Henry James, *Italian Hours*, ed. J. Auchard (Philadelphia, 1991), p. 185.
4. *Letters*, p. 129.
5. Boyd Alexander, *England's Wealthiest Son: A Study of William Beckford* (London, 1991).
6. Christie's sale catalogue, 23 January 1789.
7. Fanny Burney, *Memoirs of Dr Burney*, 3 vols. (London, 1832), vol. 3, p. 133.
8. Fanny Burney, *Diary and Letters of Madame d'Arblay, 1778–1840*, ed. Charlotte Barrett, 6 vols. (London, 1904–5), vol. 5, p. 36.
9. Public Records Office document BII/1318, Public Records Office, London.
10. *Gentleman's Magazine* vol. 69, part 1 (1799), p. 172.
11. C. B. Oldman, 'Beckford and Mozart', *Music and Letters*, 47 (1966), pp. 110–15.
12. Deutsch, p. 119.
13. Lady Anne Miller, *Letters from Italy in the Years 1770 and 1771*, 3 vols. (London, 1776), vol. 2, p. 194.

CHAPTER IX *Naples*

1. Burney, *Musical Tours*, vol. 1, p. 271.
2. *Letters*, p. 143.
3. Ibid., p. 144.
4. Ibid.
5. *Alumni Oxonienses, 1715–1886*, 4 vols. (Oxford), vol. 4, p. 1477.
6. B. Fothergill, *Sir William Hamilton: Envoy Extraordinary* (London, 1969).
7. Miller, *Letters from Italy*, vol. 2, p. 216.
8. The painting was identified in 1991 by music scholars Domenico D'Alessandro of Naples and Harrison James Wignall of Brandeis University.
9. *Letters*, p. 135. Burkhardt Shudi (1702–73) whom Leopold had known in London, was a famous harpsichord maker whose son-in-law and partner was founder of the well-known firm of Broadwood.
10. Burney, *Musical Tours*, vol. 1, p. 264.
11. *Letters*, p. 139.
12. J. W. Oliver, *The Life of William Beckford* (Oxford, 1932), p. 48.

CHAPTER X *Bologna*

1. *Letters*, p. 123.
2. P. C. Scholes, *The Great Dr Burney, His Life, His Travels, His Works, His Family and His Friends*, 2 vols. (London, 1948), vol. 1, pp. 149–50.
3. Burney, *Musical Tours*, vol. 1, p. 144.

4. Ibid., p. 146.

5. *Letters*, p. 158.

6. Burney, *Musical Tours*, vol. 1, p. 162.

7. Burney published his *Present State of Music in France and Italy* in 1771. Modern editions are edited by P. A. Scholes (1959) as *Musical Tours in Europe*, and by H. E. Poole (1974) as *Music, Men, and Manners in France and Italy*.

8. *A General History of Music, from the Earliest Ages to the Present Period* was published from 1776 to 1789 in four volumes. The present references are to the 1935 edition, edited by F. Mercer in two volumes.

9. S. Klima, G. Bowers, K. S. Grant, eds., *Memoirs of Dr Charles Burney, 1766–1769* (Lincoln, Neb., 1988), pp. 164–65.

10. Burney, vol. 2, p. 960.

11. Abraham Rees, ed., *Cyclopaedia; or Universal Dictionary of Art, Science, and Literature*, 45 vols. (1802–1819).

12. K. S. Grant, *Dr Burney as Critic and Historian of Music* (Ann Arbor, 1983), p. 792.

13. Deutsch, p. 435.

14. Grant, *Dr Burney as Critic and Historian of Music*, pp. 17–47.

CHAPTER XI *Michael Kelly*

1. Kelly, *Reminiscences*, p. 26.

2. Ibid., p. 37.

3. Ibid., p. 47.

4. Ibid., 99–103.

5. *Letters*, p. 837.

6. Kelly, *Reminiscences*, p. 104.

7. Ibid., p. 112.

8. Ibid., 112–16.

9. Ibid., 130–32.

10. Ibid., p. 129.

11. Ibid., p. 140.

12. Ibid., p. 191.

13. Ibid., p. 296.

14. J. Boaden, *Memoirs of the Life of John Phillip Kemble* (1825), 1, 350–51.

CHAPTER XII *Nancy Storace*

1. Deutsch, p. 276.

2. Betty Matthews, 'The Childhood of Nancy Storace', *Musical Times*, 101 (1969), pp. 733–35.

3. O. Michtner, *Das alte Burgtheater als Opernbühne* (Vienna, 1970), p. 150.

4. Rudolf Payer von Thurn, ed., *Joseph II als Theaterdirektor* (Vienna, 1920), p. 35.

5. *Letters*, p. 847.
6. Kelly, *Reminiscences*, p. 117–18.
7. *Letters*, p. 883.
8. Kelly, *Reminiscences*, p. 131.
9. S. M. Ellis, *The Life of Michael Kelly* (London, 1930), pp. 119–20.
10. Einstein, *Mozart: His Character, His Work*, p. 74.
11. Deutsch, p. 309.
12. Kelly, *Reminiscences*, p. 141.
13. *Letters*, p. 905.
14. Ellis, *The Life of Michael Kelly*, 149–50.
15. *Public Advertiser*, 1 March 1790.
16. A. Loewenberg, 'Some Stray Notes on Mozart', *Music and Letters* 24 (1943), pp. 164–68.
17. Jane Girdham, 'The Last of the Storaces', *Musical Times* 189 (1988), pp. 17–18.
18. Kelly, *Reminiscences*, p. 302.
19. Burney, vol. 2, p. 900.
20. *Gentleman's Magazine*, 24 August 1817.

CHAPTER XIII: *Stephen Storace*

1. Thomas Jones, *Memoirs*, Walpole Society, vol. 32 (London, 1957), 3 September 1782, p. 114.
2. Charles Burney, *Music, Men, and Manners in France and Italy*, ed. H. E. Poole, (London, 1974), p. 194.
3. Kelly, *Reminiscences*, p. 48.
4. Ibid., p. 119.
5. Roger Fiske, 'Operas of Stephen Storace', *Proceedings of the Royal Musical Association*, 86 (1959–60), pp. 29–44.
6. Kelly, *Reminiscences*, p. 122.
7. Ibid., p. 139.
8. Jane Girdham, 'A Note on Stephen Storace and Michael Kelly', *Music and Letters*, 76 (1995), pp. 66–7.
9. Letter, Add. 35538, British Museum, London.
10. Kelly, *Reminiscences*, p. 219.
11. Ibid., p. 309.
12. Quoted in Roger Fiske, 'Operas of Stephen Storace', p. 39.
13. *Letters*, p. 773.

CHAPTER XIV *Thomas Attwood, Mozart's English Pupil*

1. Mozart's income at this time seems to have been much greater than was assumed by many past biographers although his expenses were high. See Volkmar Braunbehrens, *Mozart in Vienna* (Oxford, 1991), pp. 133–41.

2. *Letters*, p. 468.

3. *Letters*, p. 893.

4. Giacomo Ferrari was a composer and harpsichordiſt. In 1792 he moved to London, where he died in 1842.

5. G. Saint-Foix, 'G. C. Ferrari, Aneddoti piacevoli e interessante', *Musical Quarterly*, 25 (1939), pp. 455–65.

6. Daniel Hertz, 'Thomas Attwood's Lessons in Composition with Mozart', *Proceedings of the Royal Musical Association*, 100 (1973–74), pp. 175–83.

7. A. Hyatt King, *Moʒart in Retrospeᵭ* (London, 1951), pp. 164–79.

8. *Letters*, p. 801.

9. Edward Holmes, *The Life of Moʒart, Including His Correspondence* (London, 1845), p. 129. Holmes was personally acquainted with Attwood.

10. Kelly, *Reminiscences*, p. 116.

11. F. G. Edwards, 'Thomas Attwood', *Musical Times* 41 (1900), pp. 788–94.

12. Cliff Eisen, *New Moʒart Documents: A Supplement to O. E. Deutsch's Documentary Biography* (London, 1991), p. 39.

13. Burney, *Memoirs of Dr Burney*, vol. 3, p. 197.

14. C. B. Oldman, 'Attwood's Dramatic Works', *Musical Times*, 107 (1966), pp. 23–25.

15. Edwards, 'Thomas Attwood', pp. 788–94.

CHAPTER XV *Invitations to England*

1. *Letters*, p. 814.

2. Ibid., p. 823.

3. Ibid., p. 817.

4. Johann Pezzl, 'Sketch of Vienna, 1786–1790', quoted in H. C. Robbins Landon, *Moʒart and Vienna* (London, 1991), p. 159.

5. Deutsch, p. 282.

6. *Letters*, p. 901.

7. Ibid., p. 904.

8. Ibid., p. 906.

9. Deutsch, p. 377.

10. Curtis Price, 'Italian Opera and Arson in Late-Eighteenth-Century London', *Journal of the American Musicological Association*, 42 (1989), pp. 55–107.

11. *Letters*, p. 945.

12. A. C. Dies, *Biographische Nachrichten von Joseph Haydn*, 1810, rev. H. Seeger (Berlin, 1959), pp. 81–83.

13. Lorenzo da Ponte, *Memorie, a cura di Giovanni Gambarin e Fauſto Nicolini*, 2 vols. (Bari, 1918), vol. 1, p. 147.

14. J. S. Jenkins, 'Mozart and Medicine in the Eighteenth Century', *Journal of the Royal Society of Medicine*, 88 (1995), pp. 408–13.

CHAPTER XVI *Vincent and Mary Novello*

1. Vincent and Mary Novello, *A Mozart Pilgrimage: Being the Travel Diaries of Vincent and Mary Novello in the Year 1829*, ed. N. Medici di Marignano and R. Hughes (London, 1955), xvii.
2. Ibid., p. 328.
3. Ibid., p. 73.
4. In the Internationale Stiftung Mozarteum, Salzburg.
5. Novello, *A Mozart Pilgrimage*, p. 85.
6. Ibid., p. 78.
7. Ibid., p. 125. Acqua toffana, a slow poison well-known in the eighteenth century, contained arsenic and lead oxide. It was said to have been invented by Tofana, a Neopolitan woman.
8. *Letters*, p. 959.
9. Novello, *A Mozart Pilgrimage*, p. 149.
10. Ibid., p. 150.
11. *Letters*, p. 784.
12. Novello, *A Mozart Pilgrimage*, p.168.
13. *Letters*, p. 340.
14. Deutsch, p. 561.

CHAPTER XVII *Mozart's Music in England after his Death*

1. Charles Burney's article on Mozart in Rees's *Cyclopaedia*.
2. Simon McVeigh, 'The Professional Concert and Rival Subscription Series in London, 1783–1793', *Royal Musical Association Research Chronicle*, 22 (1989), pp. 1–135.
3. Eisen, *New Mozart Documents*, p. 37.
4. *Morning Post and Daily Advertiser*, 14 February 1786.
5. *Daily Advertiser*, 28 March 1806.
6. A. Einstein, 'The First Performance of Mozart's Entführung in London', *Music Review*, 7 (1946), pp. 154–60.
7. M. B. Foster, *History of the Philharmonic Society of London 1813–1912* (London, 1912), p. 8.
8. A. Hyatt King, *Mozart in Retrospect* (London, 1951), pp. 115–16.
9. *Examiner*, 30 May 1819.
10. H. B. Forman ed., *Complete Works of John Keats*, 4 vols. (Glasgow, 1901), vol. 4, p. 181.
11. Edward Holmes, *The Life of Mozart, Including His Correspondence*.
12. Nicholas Temperley, 'Mozart's Influence on English Music', *Music and Letters*, 42 (1961), pp. 307–18.
13. Nicholas Temperley, 'George Frederick Pinto', *Musical Times*, 106 (1965), pp. 265–70.

14. J. K. Sterndale Bennett, *The Life of Sterndale Bennett* (Cambridge, 1907), pp. 22–25.

15. *Illustrated London News*, 12 December 1891.

16. M. B. Foster, *History of the Philharmonic Society of London*, p. 428.

17. A. Jefferson, *Sir Thomas Beecham* (London, 1979), p. 241.

Alexander, Boyd. *England's Wealthiest Son: A study of William Beckford*. London, 1991.

Alumni Oxonienses: 1715–1886. 7 vols. Oxford.

Anderson, E., ed. *The Letters of Mozart and His Family*. 3rd ed. London, 1985.

Barrington, Daines. 'An account of a remarkable young man'. *Philosophical Transactions of the Royal Society* LX (1771), pp.54–64.

Bauer, W. A., O. E. Deutsch and J. H. Eibl, eds. *Mozart: Briefe und Aufzeichnungen*. 7 vols. Kassell, 1962–75.

Beechey, Gwilym. 'Thomas Linley, Junior, 1756–1778'. *Musical Quarterly* 54 (1968), pp. 74–82.

————. 'Thomas Linley, 1756–1778, and His Vocal Music'. *Musical Times* 119 (1978), pp. 669–671.

Bennett, J. K. Sterndale. *The Life of Sterndale Bennett*. Cambridge, 1907.

Black, Clementina. *The Linleys of Bath*. London, 1971.

Boaden, J. *Memoirs of the Life of John Philip Kemble*. 2 vols. London, 1825.

Boswell, James. *Life of Johnson*. Edited by G. B. Hill. 6 vols. Oxford, 1934.

———— . *London Journal 1762–1763*. Edited by F. A. Pottle. London, 1950.

Braunbehrens, Volkmar. *Mozart in Vienna*. Oxford, 1991.

Burney, Charles. *A General History of Music from the Earliest Ages to the Present Period*. (1776–1789). Edited by F. Mercer. 2 vols. New York, 1935.

————. *Dr. Burney's Musical Tours in Europe*. Edited by P. A. Scholes. 2 vols. Oxford, 1959.

————. *Music, Men, and Manners in France and Italy*. Edited by H. E. Poole. London, 1974.

Burney, Fanny. *Diary and Letters of Madame d'Arblay, 1778–1840*. Edited by Charlotte Barrett. 6 vols. London, 1904–5.

————. *Memoirs of Dr. Burney*. 3 vols. London, 1832.

————. *Early Journals and Letters*. Edited by L. E. Troide. 3 vols. Oxford, 1988–94.

————. Evelina (1778). 2 vols. Oxford, 1968.

Da Ponte, Lorenzo. *Memorie, a cura di Giovanni Gambarin e Fausto Nicolini*. 2 vol. Bari, 1918.

De Brosses, Charles. *Lettres Familières*. Edited by G. Cafosso and L. N. Cagiano de Azevede. Naples, 1991.

Deutsch, O. E. *Mozart und seine Welt in zeitgenössischen Bildern*. Kassel, 1961.

————. *Mozart: A Documentary Biography*. Translated by E. Blom, P. Branscombe and J. Noble. 3rd ed. London, 1991.

Dies, A. C. *Biographische Nachrichten von Joseph Haydn* (1810). Revised by H. Seeger. Berlin, 1959.

Edgcumbe, Richard, Earl of Mount-Edgcumbe. *Musical Reminiscences*. 4th. ed. 1834; reprint, New York, 1973.

Edwards, F. G. 'Thomas Attwood'. *Musical Times* 41 (1900), pp. 788–94.

Einstein, A. *Mozart: His Character, His Work*. London, 1946

———. 'The First Performance of Mozart's Entführung in London'. *Music Review* 7 (1946), pp. 154–160.

Eisen, Cliff. *New Mozart Documents: A Supplement to O. E. Deutsch's Documentary Biography*. London, 1991.

Elkin, R. *The Old Concert Halls of London*. London, 1955.

Ellis, S. M. *The Life of Michael Kelly*. London, 1930.

Fiske, Roger. *English Theatre Music in the Eighteenth Century*. 2nd ed. Oxford, 1986.

———. 'Operas of Stephen Storace'. *Proceedings of Royal Musical Association* 86 (1959–60), pp. 29–44.

Forman, H. B., ed. *Complete Works of John Keats*. 4 vols. Glasgow, 1901.

Foster, M. B. *History of the Philharmonic Society of London, 1813–1912*. London, 1912.

Fothergill, B. *Sir William Hamilton: Envoy Extraordinary*. London, 1969.

Gibson, Elizabeth. 'Earl Cowper in Florence and His Correspondence with the Italian Opera in London'. *Music and Letters* 68 (1987), pp. 235–52.

Girdham, Jane. 'The Last of the Storaces'. *Musical Times* 189 (1988), pp. 17–18.

———. 'A Note on Stephen Storace and Michael Kelly'. *Music and Letters* 76 (1995), pp. 66–67.

Grant, K. S. *Dr. Burney as Critic and Historian of Music*. Ann Arbor, Mich., 1983.

Hertz, David. 'Thomas Attwood's Lessons in Composition with Mozart'. *Proceedings of the Royal Musical Association* 100 (1973–74), pp. 175–83.

Highfill, P. H., K. A. Burnim and E. A. Langhans. *A Biographical Dictionary of Actors, Actresses, Musicians, Dancers, Managers and Other Stage Personnel in London, 1660–1800*. Carbondale, Ill., 1973–93.

Holmes, Edward. *The Life of Mozart, Including his Correspondence*. London, 1845.

Jackson, William. *The Leisure Hour*. London, 1882.

James, Henry. *Italian Hours*. Edited by J. Auchard. Philadelphia, 1991.

Jefferson, A. *Sir Thomas Beecham*. London, 1979.

Jenkins, J. S. 'Mozart and Medicine in the Eighteenth Century'. *Journal of the Royal Society of Medicine* 88 (1995), pp 408–13.

———. 'Leopold Mozart. A Patient in Eighteenth-Century London'. *Journal of Medical Biography* 5 (1997), pp. 30–32.

Johnstone, H. Dyack, and Roger Fiske. *Music in Britain: The Eighteenth Century*. Oxford, 1990.

Jones, Thomas. *Memoirs*. Walpole Society. Vol. 32. London, 1951.

Kelly, Michael. *Reminiscences*. Edited by Roger Fiske. Oxford, 1975.

King, A. Hyatt. *Mozart in Retrospect*. London, 1951.

———. *A Mozart Legacy*. London, 1984.

Klima, S., G. Bowers and K. S. Grant, eds. *Memoirs of Dr. Charles Burney, 1766–1769*. Lincoln, Neb., 1988.

Landon, H. C. Robbins. *Mozart and Vienna*. London, 1991.

Lee, Vernon. *Studies of the Eighteenth Century in Italy*. London, 1907.

Loewenberg, Alfred. 'Some Stray Notes on Mozart'. *Music and Letters* 24 (1943), pp. 164–68.

McVeigh, Simon. *Concert Life in London from Mozart to Haydn*. Cambridge, 1993.

———. 'Felice Giardini: A Violinist in Eighteenth Century London'. *Music and Letters* 64 (1983), pp. 162–72.

———. 'The Professional Concert and Rival Subscription Series in London, 1783–1793'. *Royal Musical Association Research Chronicle* 22 (1989), pp. 1–135.

Malmesbury, Earl of, ed. *A Series of Letters of 1st Earl of Malmesbury, Family, and Friends from 1745 to 1820*. 2 vols. London, 1870.

Matthews, Betty. 'The Childhood of Nancy Storace'. *Musical Times* 101 (1969), pp. 733–35.

Michtner, O. *Das alte Burgtheater als Opernbühne*. Vienna, 1970.

Miller, Lady Anne. *Letters from Italy in the Years 1770 and 1771*. 3 vols. London, 1776.

Nissen, G. N. von. *Biographie W. A. Mozarts*. Leipzig, 1828; reprint, 1964.

Nottebohm, G. *Mozartiana*. Leipzig, 1880.

Novello, Vincent and Mary. *A Mozart Pilgrimage: Being the Travel Diaries of Vincent and Mary Novello in the Year 1829*. Edited by N. Medici di Marignano and R. Hughes. London, 1955.

Oldman, C. B. 'Atwood's Dramatic Works'. *Musical Times* 107 (1966), pp. 23–5.

———. 'Beckford and Mozart'. *Music and Letters* 47 (1966), pp. 110–15.

Oliver, J. W. *The Life of William Beckford*. Oxford, 1932.

Papendiek, Charlotte L. H. *Court and Private Life in the Time of Queen Charlotte: Being the Journals of Mrs Papendiek*. Edited by Mrs. V. D. Broughton. 2 vols. London, 1887.

Payer von Thurn, Rudolf, ed. *Joseph II als Theaterdirektor*. Vienna, 1920.

Pepys, Samuel. *Diary*. Edited by R. Latham and W. Matthews. 11 vols. London, 1970–83.

Pohl, C. F. *Mozart and Haydn in England*. 2 vols. Vienna, 1867.

Price, Curtis. 'Italian Opera and Arson in Late Eighteenth Century London'. *Journal of the American Musicological Association* 42 (1989), pp. 55–107.

Rees, Abraham, ed. *Cyclopaedia; or Universal Dictionary of Art, Science and Literature*. 45 vols. London, 1802–19.

Roe, S. 'J. C. Bach, 1735–1782: Towards a New Biography'. *Musical Times* 123 (1982), pp. 23–6.

Roscoe, C. 'Two Eighteenth-Century Non-Events'. *Musical Times* 112 (1971), pp. 18–19.

Saint-Foix, G. de. 'G. C. Ferrari., Aneddoti piacevoli e interessante'. *Musical Quarterly* 25 (1939), pp. 455–65.

Scholes, P. C. *The Great Dr. Burney. His Life, His Travels, His Works, His Family and His Friends.* 2 vols. London, 1948.

Smollett, Tobias. *Travels Through France and Italy* (1766). Oxford, 1981.

————. *Humphrey Clinker* (1771). Oxford, 1984.

Terry, C. S. *John Christian Bach.* Revised by H. C. Robbins. 2nd ed. London, 1967.

Temperley, Nicholas. 'Mozart's Influence on English Music'. *Music and Letters* 42 (1961), pp. 307–18.

Temperley, Nicholas. 'George Frederick Pinto'. *Musical Times* 106 (1965), pp. 265–70.

Walpole, Horace. *Horace Walpole's Correspondence.* Edited by S. Lewis. 48 vols. London and Oxford, 1937–83.

Warburton, Ernest. 'J. C. Bach's Operas'. *Proceedings of the Royal Musical Association* 92 (1965–66), pp. 95–106.

Woodall, Mary, ed. *The Letters of Thomas Gainsborough.* Revised ed. 1963.

Woodfield, I. 'New Light on the Mozarts' London Visit'. *Music and Letters* 76 (1995), pp. 187–208.

Zaslaw, N. and W. Cowdery. *The Compleat Mozart.* New York, 1990.

INDEX